THE LAST
SECRET
— OF —
FATIMA

THE LAST SECRET OF FATIMA

MY CONVERSATIONS WITH SISTER LUCIA

CARDINAL TARCISIO BERTONE

WITH GIUSEPPE DE CARLI

FOREWORD BY

POPE BENEDICT XVI

DOUBLEDAY

NEW YORK   LONDON   TORONTO   SYDNEY   AUCKLAND

PUBLISHED BY DOUBLEDAY

English translation copyright © 2008 by Doubleday, a division of Random House, Inc.

All Rights Reserved

Published in the United States by Doubleday, an imprint of The Doubleday Broadway Publishing Group, a division of Random House, Inc., New York.
www.doubleday.com

DOUBLEDAY and the portrayal of an anchor with a dolphin are registered trademarks of Random House, Inc.

Originally published in Italy as *L' Ultima veggente di Fatima* by RCS Libri S.p.A., Milan, in 2007. Copyright © 2007 RCS Libri S.p.A, Milano. This edition published by arrangement with RCS Libri S.p.A.

Book design by Ruth Lee

Library of Congress Cataloging-in-Publication Data
Bertone, Tarcisio.
The last secret of Fatima : my conversations with Sister Lucia / Tarcisio Bertone ; with Giuseppe De Carli ; foreword by Pope Benedict XVI.
p. cm.
Includes bibliographical references and index.
1. Fatima, Our Lady of. 2. Mary, Blessed Virgin, Saint—Apparitions and miracles—Portugal—Fatima. 3. Mary, Blessed Virgin, Saint—Prophecies. 4. Maria Lúcia, Irmã, 1907–2005. I. De Carli, Giuseppe, 1952– II. Title.
BT660.F3B37 2008
232.91'70946945—dc22
2007050548

ISBN 978-0-385-52582-4

PRINTED IN THE UNITED STATES OF AMERICA

1   3   5   7   9   10   8   6   4   2

First Edition in the United States of America

To John Paul II, the Pope of Fatima

To Benedict XVI, the Pope of the Black Madonna of Altötting

CONTENTS

Part Two

MESSAGES, INTERPRETATIONS, AND ACTS OF ENTRUSTMENT

FOREWORD BY POPE BENEDICT XVI

TO His Eminence
   Cardinal Tarcisio Bertone
   Secretary of State

Venerable Brother, you have entrusted so many memories to the pages of your book, *L'ultima veggente di Fatima,* in order that they may not be just a precious baggage of personal emotions but might be consigned to the collective memory as meaningful traces of the Church's age-old history, since they deal with events which marked her in the last part of the twentieth century.

In fact, we both lived the chapter that addresses the publication of the third part of the Secret of Fatima in that memorable time of the Great Jubilee of the Year 2000: I, in my capacity as prefect of the Congregation for the Doctrine of the Faith, and you, as secretary of the same dicastery.

John Paul II, the great pontiff who preceded me, who was a font of prophetic inspirations and was personally convinced that it was "the motherly hand" of the Virgin who had diverted the bullet that might have killed him, realized that the time had come to dispel the air of mystery that shrouded the last part of the secret that the Virgin has entrusted to the three little shepherd children of Fatima. The Congregation for the Doctrine of the Faith, which preserved the precious document written by Sr. Lucia, was made responsible for doing so.

It was time for illumination, not only so that the message could be known by all, but also so that the truth could be revealed amid the confused apocalyptic interpretations and speculation that were circulating in the Church, disturbing the faithful rather than inviting them to prayer and penance.

Nevertheless, on the other hand, it was possible to see around the impressive Shrine the comforting development of Marian piety. This authentic source of Christian life, which had sprung up in Fatima and in every part of the world where devotion to the Virgin under the influence of the apparitions at Fatima was deeply rooted in the popular faith, was an invitation to men and women to consecrate themselves to the Immaculate Heart of Mary.

The conversations between the seer, the last survivor of the three little shepherds, and you as the bishop sent by the pope, were not only an important ascertainment of the truthfulness of the events but also an opportunity for you to become acquainted with Sr. Lucia's transparent soul and her heartfelt intelligence typical of her femininity, which had been translated into a strong Christian faith. In addition, through the experiences of this humble sister, the role of the Virgin Mary shines forth, who gives Christians a motherly hand in the trials and tribulations of life.

I myself wrote the "Theological Commentary" on the event, after having prayed intensely and meditated profoundly on the authentic words of the third part of the secret of Fatima contained in the pages written by Sr. Lucia. I was impressed by the comforting promise of the Virgin Most Holy, as a synthesis and a precious seal to it: "My Immaculate Heart will triumph." [1]

As I wrote: "The *fiat* of Mary, the word of her heart, has changed the history of the world, because it brought the Savior into the world—because, thanks to her *Yes*, God could become man in our world and remains so for all time."

And further, "But since God himself took a human heart and has thus steered human freedom toward what is good, the freedom to choose evil no longer has the last word."[2] The message of Fatima is a further proof of this.

I invoke upon all who approach the testimony offered in this book, the protection of Our Blessed Lady of Fatima, and I impart my Apostolic Blessing to you, Your Eminence, and to Dr. Giuseppe De Carli, who shared with you the toil of drafting these memoirs.[3]

From the Vatican, February 22, 2007
Pope Benedict XVI

A NOTE TO THE READER

The medieval Latin authors have given us a term that is helpful for understanding what this book attempts to accomplish: *manuductio.* The twelfth-century writer John of Salisbury uses the term in the sense of "safe conduct." In a more high-flown literary register, *manuductio* means "the act of leading by the hand." In this latter usage, the word refers to the author's method of guiding his reader toward understanding the meaning of the text.

Our *manuductio* in this book is offered by Cardinal Tarcisio Bertone, who, while still secretary of the Congregation for the Doctrine of the Faith, was sent by Pope John Paul II to meet with Sister Lucia, the last visionary of Fatima, in her Coimbra convent. His assignment was to verify in conversation with her the genuineness and reliability of the text of the so-called Third Secret. The cardinal's errand was evidence of the eager interest of a pope who had become increasingly convinced that he was called to a mission of suffering. John Paul II interpreted the shooting as a sign. (After all, until the assassination attempt, everyone would have dismissed a prediction of a bullet in Saint Peter's Square as, well, some apocalyptic prophecy.) In an impromptu Angelus address delivered from the window of his study after an operation for a fractured femur, the pope gave powerful expression to his conviction that he had been called to suffer: "The pope had to suffer. . . . There is a higher Gospel, and it is the Gospel of suffering." Not only does the martyrdom of the twentieth-century Church coalesce, like coagulating blood, around the figure of John Paul II, but his personal story as pope took a supernatural turn precisely at a time when the secular utopian ideologies were in full retreat.

Cardinal Bertone's story is a work in progress, but it has the advantage of clarity. In contrast to the cloud of interpretations swirling around the message Our Lady delivered to the three shepherd children in 1917, his testimony in this book puts the final seal on the definitive version of the events. Expressions of doubt are notably absent from the account that follows. Rather, we find phrases such as "I am certain," "Lucia confirmed," and "her memory was absolutely accurate." Among the many mysteries unveiled in this book, we learn about the secret meetings between Cardinal Bertone and a nun who for decades had knocked mostly in vain at the door of the Vatican. Sometimes the shortest distance between two points is, well, an arabesque. Not this time, though; here it is a straight line that drives right into the heart of the issues. Cardinal Bertone's notes reveal to us the real Lucia, whom the cardinal describes as a persistent, stubborn, exuberant Carmelite nun. And through Lucia we are transported back to the Cova da Iria, where we become playmates of the three children whose lives were powerfully touched by the divine. Lucia is the leader of the group, the one who listens and explains. Similarly, it is Lucia who writes "despite the repugnance I feel, I will obey"; who reveals connections that can't be mere coincidences or literary inventions; who—through the words of Cardinal Bertone—introduces us to the "meta-story" of Fatima and sets aside once and for all the suspicions that the Fatima texts were doctored to hide the truth. With guides like these, we need have no anxiety about ending up lost in a "dark wood of error." On the contrary, we can be confident that our journey will lead us back, almost by magic, to the extraordinary, poetic atmosphere we encounter whenever the sacred invades a truly open mind with its superhuman presence.

In the following pages, Cardinal Bertone shares with us his amazement over Lucia as a person. But he also invites us to join him in a deeper exploration of the greatness of the pontificate of John Paul II, the Pope of Fatima (and the pope of *Dominus Iesus,* just to be clear), the pope of "suffering and silence," as Benedict XVI described him.[1] Fatima stands for the gift of a more mature faith, a faith that is not ashamed to give a broader scope to the emotions (which suggests one reason that Our Lady is the central personage in the majority of apparitions). Nevertheless, the following pages are not just about Fatima. They contain, for instance, a critical reflection on Medjugorje, and they revisit a significant portion of the pontificate of Benedict XVI (the conclave and the election, Benedict's role as "catechist to the world," the Regensburg lecture, his amazing trip to Turkey). Above all, though, this book is an effort to make the reader better acquainted with the heavenly messenger herself, that is, to understand the identity of Mary. We all know that fervor often mutates into gushing enthusiasm and that feeling can take the place of faith. It is tempting to exploit the extraordinary in order to glut the spiritual curiosity of the masses. Cardinal Bertone's calm and judicious mind offers us a powerful antidote to this temptation.

Cardinal Bertone's story sheds a whole new light on the phenomenon of pilgrimages to Marian shrines. These pilgrimages are a form of prayer on the move. They begin with a radical decision: "Go from your country and your kindred and your father's house to the land that I will show you" (Gen. 12:1). In other words: Leave your home and set off, with an open heart, to a holy place where you can meet God. It is Abraham's response to this call, after his encounter with Yahweh, that marks the beginning of the whole history of salvation. The very fact of departing is already a victory over the inertia of habit; it is a break with all our customary mediocrity, a decision to set out on a path of forgotten demands and sacrifices. In a word: The cardinal's story helps us remember that the journey to the holy place is an expression of eschatological hope.

The pilgrim's journey is also a key to unlocking the unsuspected depths of the mystery of penance, which Our Lady insists upon in the Third Secret. Fatima reminds us that penance is not at all the trivial, petty sideline to which it is too often reduced, and Fatima helps us recover the forgotten meaning of penance as an act of conversion, as a return to the gushing springs of life. "Behold, I am the handmaid of the Lord" (Lk 1:38). "My soul magnifies the Lord" (Lk 1:46). What could be a more dumbfounding contrast to the fog of bloodless language that has settled over modern Christianity than the experience of the three shepherd children? They learned how to approach the Virgin by watching her, by contemplating her radiant childlikeness, which is unclouded by the slightest trace of vanity. Beholding her smile, they smiled back, just like a baby who comes to know its mother even before learning her name. French novelist Georges Bernanos describes the Virgin's gaze in these words: "It is not the look of indulgence . . . but of tender compassion, pained surprise. It is the look that reveals the inconceivable purity which makes her younger than sin, younger than the race from which she has sprung. Though she is the mother for and of grace, she is also the youngest member of the human race."[2] Does this book offer us a *manuductio ad coelum,* "a helping hand to heaven," to borrow the terminology of the seventeenth-century Cistercian Cardinal Giovanni Bona? Perhaps. Unless your heart is made of stone and your mind is completely jaded, certain subjects inevitably inspire you to look a little higher and a little further than you did before.

Grateful acknowledgments are in order for this little spiritual enterprise. I would like to thank Father Luis Kondor, SVD, vice-postulator of the cause for the beatification of Jacinta and Francisco; the Secretariado dos Pastorinhos, especially Father Luciano Coelho Cristino, who works in the office of study and promotion; the Mariologist Stefano De Fiores;

Don Claudio Rossini, director of the Libreria Editrice Vaticana; Father Giuseppe Colombara, photography editor of *L'Osservatore Romano;* Carinal Bertone's faithful team in the Secretariat of State of the Holy See; Giuseppe Marchetti Tricamo, director of Rai-Eri; Lucia Gradi; and, finally, Pasquale Faccia, a peerless advisor in the composition of these pages.

THE LAST
SECRET
—— OF ——
FATIMA

INTRODUCTION

Under the Mantle of Mary

"Your Eminence, wouldn't it be a great idea to do a book on your meetings with Sister Lucia, the last of the Fatima visionaries? Wouldn't it greatly benefit both potential readers and the millions of people around the world who are devoted to Mary? Wouldn't it give us an insight into this nun who was a thorn in the side of practically every twentieth-century pope? Wouldn't an account of your meetings with Lucia give us an opportunity to become better acquainted with her? Wouldn't it give us a deeper insight into the amazing adventure that befell her and her two young cousins, Jacinta and Francisco, in 1917?"

As I peppered him with this machine-gun fire of questions, Cardinal Tarcisio Bertone, at the time still Archbishop of Genoa, looked at me with the harried attention that tends to appear on the face of every bishop weighed down to the point of physical exhaustion by a heavy schedule. Cardinal Bertone was already stepping into his car, and the eyes of his secretary, Father Stefano, were flashing with impatience.

The cardinal and I were just coming from a one-day conference entitled "From John Paul II to Benedict XVI," where we had been the two main presenters. We had reminisced fondly about John Paul II, the "great Apostle of the Rosary,"[1] as Benedict XVI has called his predecessor in a recent Angelus address. Benedict went on in the same address to describe John Paul II as the pope whom "we remember . . . on his knees, his rosary beads in his hands, immersed in the contemplation of Christ as he himself invited us to do in his Apostolic Letter *Rosarium Virginis Mariae*."[2]

We could also say that Karol Wojtyla was the pope of the Marian shrines. He outdid every previous pontiff in the number of pilgrimages he undertook to the sanctuaries where Mary is honored. He was intimately familiar with this special landscape in the geography of grace. Every one of his apostolic journeys included a moment set aside for the Blessed Mother. You would see John Paul II kneeling before a statue of the Virgin, or crowning an image of the Madonna in some city square, or even consecrating a place of worship in her honor, such as the shrine of Our Lady of Peace in Yamassoukro on the Ivory Coast, which is nicknamed the "Saint Peter's of the Savannah." John Paul II's pontificate unfolded under the mantle of Mary; it was one long chain of what he liked to call "acts of entrustment" to the Blessed Virgin. In short, John Paul II was Mary's pope.

It was therefore fitting that the last of John Paul's 104 apostolic journeys outside Italy was his visit to Lourdes in August 2004. In some sense, this trip closed a mysterious circle that had begun on May 13, 1981, with the wounds inflicted on the pope by his would-be assassin. The fact that John Paul II survived the shooting would in turn have an (at the time) unforeseeable political consequence: the collapse of the Berlin Wall and the dissolution of the USSR. Having alluded to these events, we come to John Paul II's connection with Fatima.

John Paul II was undeniably the Pope of Fatima. He revealed the Third Secret and applied to himself its prophecy concerning the "Bishop dressed in White," who falls before a big cross under a rain of bullets and arrows. This image sums up the experience of the twentieth-century popes, who were forced to lead the Church along a Via Crucis strewn with the corpses of the martyrs. Stalin once asked, "How many divisions

does the pope have?" At Fatima, Our Lady seemed to offer an unequivocally clear response: The pope's divisions are the millions of unarmed
Christians who have sacrificed their lives for the sake of Christ and the
Church. The geopolitical scene has completely changed since Stalin's
time, and it would seem that the pope's divisions have won the struggle.

At the conference I mentioned (which took place at Opus Dei's house
for college students in Genoa's Albano district), Cardinal Bertone and I
explored the experience of John Paul II from our different points of
view. This great pope lived at the point where time and eternity intersect
to form a cross. And this cross brought John Paul II not only salvation,
but also pain, defeat, and mysterious agony. At a certain point during the
proceedings, the cardinal said: "I could tell you a lot about Sister Lucia,
about how she received me, about her relationship with the Holy Father,
and about how her encounter with Our Lady changed her life." Cardinal
Bertone said this in passing, and the momentum of the conference carried us on to other topics. Nevertheless, his remark seared big fiery letters in my brain. "I could tell you a lot," he said. My first reaction was:
"Well, if you can tell it, then maybe you can write it down, too." When I
verbalized this thought to him, the cardinal replied: "Let me think about
it. I don't have a lot of time, but I did take some notes of my meetings
with Sister Lucia. Who knows, maybe it might . . ." He never finished the
sentence. The car whisked him off to his next appointment through
Genoa's steep, narrow streets. All I had to go on was a hint of willingness
on Cardinal Bertone's part. Should I pursue my idea or should I drop it?

A PERFECT POSTMODERN MIX

I was daunted by the topic, even though I had narrowed down the focus
of my research to manageable proportions. My goal was to discover the
personal character of Sister Lucia through the living memory and testimony of Cardinal Tarcisio Bertone. I hoped that Lucia in her turn would

connect me with the most significant revelation of the twentieth century, a revelation whose impact reached far beyond the world of spirituality.

Admittedly, I wasn't exactly a complete novice. I had been in Fatima on May 13, 2000, to cover the beatification of Jacinta and Francisco for Italian TV. I had felt a thrill of emotion as I translated for my viewers Cardinal Angelo Sodano's closing address (in Portuguese), in which he announced the pope's intention to publish the Third Secret. Then, on June 26, 2000, Bishop Rino Fisichella and I had covered the presentation of the Third Secret for Italy's Rai television network (the event actually took place in the Holy See's packed press room; we followed it by live video link from the Rai studios in Rome's Borgo Sant'Angelo district). The presenters were Cardinal Joseph Ratzinger, at the time prefect of the Congregation for the Doctrine of the Faith; and Archbishop Tarcisio Bertone, Ratzinger's then second-in-command at the CDF. The press conference harnessed the inventions of the electronic age in the service of a mystery replete with devils, hell, and prophetic visions. It was a perfect postmodern mix—just the thing for a postmodern pope such as John Paul II. An apt title for the event would have been something like "Fatima, Secret of Blood." The press conference was a masterful fusion of powerful symbolism and mass-media savvy.

Did I say I was daunted by the topic? You bet I was. To write about Fatima means to deal with phenomena such as apparitions, miracles, children offering their lives for the conversion of sinners, destruction and mayhem, the martyrdom of the good, the consecration of Russia, and shining angels who pour water out of a crystal jar onto the souls who approach God, not to mention the trembling, uncertain step of a pope ("the Bishop dressed in White"). All of this is enough to make your head spin. I don't know how many times I told myself that it's only in complete silence that you can begin to listen, and that it's only when language ceases that you can begin to see.

Numerous articles about the revelation of the Third Secret appeared around the time of its official publication, but there was one that struck me in particular. The author was a Jewish atheist writer, Marek Halter. "The thing that made Moses great," Halter wrote,

> was his humanity. Actually, it was the fact that he died like a human being. After the failed attempt to assassinate John Paul II, which had been foreseen by the Fatima visionaries, the Pope could have immediately divulged the secret in order to pass himself off as a saint among the faithful. Instead, he concealed the prophecy as long as he could, because he wanted to die like a human being, just like Moses. That is the deep truth of Fatima.

Halter's words hit me like a bolt of lightning. They brought home to me the necessity of proceeding humbly and resisting every urge for sensationalism. Sensationalism may be the bread and butter of journalism (and religious salesmanship), but it's like replacing the inward light of the soul with the outward flash of a neon billboard. Fatima, I realized, isn't some sensational spectacle; it's a deep, yet light-filled mystery. So I decided to pursue my project, while maintaining the requisite respect and discretion. I wrote cards, made telephone calls, and even sent a few e-mails to Archbishop Bertone's personal secretary. One day, I finally got a reply. But I'll come back to that later.

In the meantime, I had two problems to tackle. The first was posed by the endless body of literature on apparitions. Interestingly, though, it is only recently that the topic has begun to register on the theological radar. Apparitions are still mostly studied by the human sciences, which approach them as psychological or paranormal phenomena. Nevertheless, as the number of apparitions, real or alleged, has increased, the subject has gradually begun to claim the attention of theologians as well.

Clearly, apparitions fall under the category of what are called *private revelations*, which add nothing to the *sola Scriptura* (Scripture alone), the only revelation deserving of faith in the strict theological sense. On this point, Luther and Saint John of the Cross join hands across the gulf that otherwise separates their respective creeds. Of course, Saint John, being faithful to Catholic teaching, adds the Church's living tradition as a source for the knowledge of Revelation. Dante skillfully summarizes the same position in three lines of the *Divine Comedy:*

> *You have the New and the Old Testament/*
> *and the pastor of the Church to guide you:/*
> *seek nothing further for your salvation.*[3]

Judged by this criterion, apparitions are marginal epiphenomena.

Some theologians, though, have gone to the opposite extreme. In their enthusiasm for apparitions, they have tried to mount an interdisciplinary argument to show that these phenomena, which some consider to be secondary, are actually a "prophetic charism" that our age chooses to ignore at its own peril. According to these theologians, apparitions are a challenge to the culture, especially to our Western culture, which they say is corroded by secularism and by an increasingly pronounced indifference toward anything that can't be perceived by the senses. Among this second group of theologians are authors such as Yves Marie Cardinal Congar, Billet, Karl Rahner, René Laurentin, Hans Urs von Balthasar, Eugen Drewermann, Rosino Gibellini, Seveau, and many, many others whose work I came across in the course of my research.

If I had to sum up the fruit of my study of the theology of apparitions, I wouldn't be able to do much better than a patchwork of learned but inconclusive citations representing a bewildering variety of schools and sub-schools. As I read up on Fatima, I was asked to accept any number of supposedly invincible theories that in fact do not stand up to the hammer of criticism or, to put it in a more down-to-earth fashion, to common sense, active discernment, cautious openness, or intelligent acceptance. I would like to cite Stefano De Fiores, an exceptionally balanced Mariologist, whose book *Maria: Nuovissimo Dizionario* I unhesitatingly recommend to anyone considering an ascent of these lofty theological peaks:

> In interpreting Marian apparitions, all we can do is gratefully accept the charism of the visionaries and try to grasp the deeper significance of the events to which they bear witness. Apparitions have a profound meaning that concerns the past, the present, and the future. They highlight the person and role of Mary as presented in the Bible, which transmits the true and fundamental Marian apparition. Apparitions also draw attention to Mary's mission as a mother who is always present to her children and never leaves their side. Apparitions reveal her as the merciful sign of divine love, as a source of life and grace. When the Virgin's messages sound an apocalyptic note, they prepare the Church for the future, inspiring it with the fighting spirit it will need for the coming pitched battle between good and evil.[4]

Though this is definitely not journalistic language, a journalist who wants to deal with this sort of topic is certainly on safe ground when he follows the lead of experts of the caliber of De Flores. He won't feel as if the earth were about to cave in under his feet, or that he is about to expose himself to the ridicule of every passerby.

Mary is a "merciful sign of divine love." Cardinal Bertone is right when he says in the interview that follows that we need to rediscover the importance of a maternal faith that is not afraid of the emotions. We need a mother. As he opened the Holy Door at the Basilica of Saint Mary Major, John Paul II exclaimed: "The story of every human being is written first of all in the heart of his own mother. No wonder, then, that the same thing was true of the earthly life-story of the Son of God."

An Illiterate Forced to Write

The second problem I faced had to do with the complex nature of Sister Lucia's activity as a writer. Though Lucia benefited from little formal education, she wrote a great deal, despite frequent assertions to the contrary. She never wrote willingly, but always took up the pen because she felt commanded to: either by Our Lady, who appeared to her often throughout her almost hundred years on earth (she died on February 13, 2005, at the age of ninety-seven), or else by her superiors, such as bishops, confessors, or other priests. She sent many letters to the Vatican and wrote directly to the popes; she corresponded with hundreds of people. Admittedly, she had no confidence in her ability to express herself properly, and she often confessed her own inadequacy. Once she even said— and this is a literal quote—"not even my handwriting is correct." In spite of this, she spent almost seventy years of her life recording her memories in writing. Her style is like a smooth surface rippled by the occasional breath of lyricism. She writes simply, even elegantly and subtly; at times she is even ironic, at least with regard to herself. We know Lucia was a nun privileged with extraordinary experiences. Her character as a writer, however, is a practically unknown aspect of her identity.

As Lucia's personality and her faith matured, and as she grew more confident in her mastery of the art of writing, her perception of the world took on new depth. Her self-knowledge became increasingly clear, just as her awareness of her own experience became ever more transparent—notwithstanding moments of panic and doubt, or the occasional suspicion of her inadequacy to capture her infinite, ineffable subject matter within the limits of human language. As Lucia grew, she published new editions of her memoirs. Each successive version contained an addition, a new intuition, a new window onto the supernatural, or a fresh detail hitherto buried in the storeroom of her memory. There are indeed "more things in heaven and earth . . . than are dreamt of in [our] philosophy," and it is not easy for those touched by the finger of God to talk about them.

Where to start? I think of four books here: Sister Lucia's memoirs, in the third edition, translated as *Fatima in Lucia's Own Words: Sister Lucia's Memoirs* (Coimbra: Grafica da Coimbra, 1998); *Calls from the Message of Fatima* (Still River, Mass.: Ravengate Press, 2005); Sister Lucia's last literary effort, *Come vedo il Messaggio di Fatima nel corso del tempo e degli avvenimenti* (Coimbra: Edizioni Carmelo di Coimbra—Segretariato dei Pastorelli, 2006); finally, *In Memoria di Suor Lucia,* by Sister Maria Celina of Jesus Crucified, the prioress of Lucia's convent in Coimbra, Portugal (Coimbra: Edizioni Carmelo di Coimbra—Segretariato dei Pastorelli, 2005). These books are all composed in the same style, which, though not fancy, is hardly banal. Listen, for example, to this passage from the Fourth Memoir:

> I am writing in a hidden corner of the attic, in the light peering through a shabby windowpane. I have retreated here in order to escape human eyes as far as I can. My table is my knees and my chair is an old suitcase. Why don't you write in your cell? someone will say. The Lord wished to deprive me even of my cell, although there are a lot of empty ones in this house. And that is fine. I don't need anything else except obedience and abandonment to God's work in me. The truth is that I am nothing but a poor, miserable tool that he has chosen to use. The painter, when he's done with his paintbrush, throws it into the fire where it is reduced to ashes. Similarly, it won't be long before the heavenly Father finishes with his instrument and reduces it to the ash of the tomb, where it will lie until the great day of the eternal alleluia. I do ardently wish for that day. You see, the tomb is not an ultimate destruction, but the beginning of the happiness of eternal and infinite love.

Sister Lucia seems to straddle the boundary between a spirituality that looks at God only in terms of how he can help the world and a spirituality that looks at the world only in terms of how it can help lead us to God. The difference between these two approaches is a matter of where the heart's priorities lie. If you think about it, though, the second approach is actually the same thing as Christianity pure and simple, and any attempt to justify or explain Christianity succeeds only in diminishing or adulterating it. I don't know whether Sister Lucia was familiar with the work of that other great lover of Mary—Saint Bernard of Clairvaux. But in one of her memoirs, she does cite the hymn *Jesu Dulcis Memoria,* which comes out of the Cistercian tradition and distills the essence of Bernard's experience: "Neither tongue nor word can express it; only one who has experienced can understand what it means to love Jesus" *(Nec lingua potest dicere, nec littera exprimere; expertus novit tenere, / quid sit Jesum diligere).*

THE FATEFUL NUMBER THIRTEEN

Fatima is not an isolated phenomenon. Far be it from me to question whether Mary's various messages are consistent with one another or whether they pursue a common "strategy." Ironically, it was just when the theologians had finished demoting visions to second-class phenomena that the era of the major apparitions began. Paray-le-Monial and Saint Margaret Mary Alacoque (1673–1675); the Marian apparitions at Rue du Bac in Paris (1830), La Salette (1846), Lourdes (1858), Pontmain (1871), Fatima (1917), Beauraing (1932–1933), Banneaux (1933). Billet reckons that between 1928 and 1975 there were 232 authentic and alleged apparitions in thirty-two countries, with the tide of phenomena hitting its peak sometime between 1954 and 1957. Speaking through the respective diocesan bishops, the Church has recognized only 15 of these occurrences as authentic. Among them are 11 apparitions: Rome, 1842 (Maria Alphonse Ratisbonne sees the Virgin); La Salette, 1846 (apparitions of the Virgin to Maximin and Mélanie); Rimini, Italy, 1850 (an image of the *Mater Misericordiae* whose eyes move for several days); Taggia, Italy, 1855 (a statue of Our Lady whose eyes move several times); Lourdes, 1858 (eighteen apparitions to Bernadette Soubirous); Pontmain, France, 1871 (Mary appears to Eugène Barbette); Gietrzwald, Poland, 1877 (two girls see the Virgin); Quito, Ecuador, 1906 (the image of Our Lady of Good Success moves its eyes more than twenty times); Fatima, 1917 (six apparitions of Mary); Beauraing, Belgium, 1932–1933 (thirty-three apparitions to five children); Banneaux, Belgium, 1933 (eight apparitions to the twelve-year-old girl Mariette Béco); Siracusa, Italy, 1953 (an image of the Immaculate Heart of Mary weeps for four days); Zaytun, Egypt, 1968 (the Mother of Light appears several times on the dome of a Coptic church); Akita, Japan, 1973 (a statue of Our Lady weeps 101 times); Kibeho, Rwanda, 1981–1989 (Our Lady appears to seven visionaries).

Stefano De Fiores points out that Fatima differs from all the other approved Marian apparitions in four respects. First, in her other apparitions, Mary recommends individual practices of piety, but at Fatima she presented a whole spirituality centered on devotion to her Immaculate Heart. Second, the other apparitions mainly have to do with spirituality, but Fatima was also concerned with political history; Mary talks about war and peace, and she warns against the devastating effects of Russian communism and state-imposed atheism. Third, in each of the other cases Mary appears just a few times, but Our Lady of Fatima extended her dialogue with humanity over almost a full century; even after 1917 she spoke to and through Sister Lucia, who explained, completed, and confirmed the message given to the three shepherd children. Fourth, the influence of the other apparitions is geographically limited, but Fatima has had a universal influence on the piety of the faithful, of the bishops, and even of the popes—especially of John Paul II, who believed Our Lady had thwarted the assassination attempt that almost claimed his life.

John Paul II was shot on May 13, 1981, but thirteen is a number that seems to have been fated to play a role in the life of more than just this one pope. Pius IX, the pope who proclaimed the dogma of the Immaculate Conception, was born on May 13, 1792. Pius XII, who proclaimed the dogma of the Assumption, was consecrated bishop by Pope Benedict XV on May 13, 1917—the same day that Mary first appeared to Lucia, Jacinta, and Francisco. The same Pope Pius XII also chose Fatima as the site for the official conclusion of the Holy Year that was celebrated in 1950. Fatima, or Sister Lucia, also played a role in the life of Pope John XXIII. As we are informed by archival records, Father Pierre Paul Philippe, OP, acting on the authority of Alfredo Cardinal Ottaviani, brought the envelope containing the Third Secret to the papal apartments, where John XXIII opened it on August 17, 1959. Paul VI met with Sister Lucia during his pilgrimage to Fatima in 1967. But it was Pope John Paul II who put his seal on the whole amazing story. The number thirteen would keep coming up at every stage of his pontificate.

As I just noted, John Paul II was shot on May 13, 1981. He beatified the shepherd children, Jacinta and Francisco, on May 13, 2003. Ali Agca was extradited to Turkey on June 13, 2003. Sister Lucia died on February 13, 2005. John Paul II himself passed away on April 2, 2005 (the numbers in the date add up to thirteen) at 21:37 in the evening (these numbers add up to thirteen, too). Finally, on May 13, 2005, Benedict XVI announced the opening of canonization proceedings for John Paul II in the Saint John Lateran Basilica.

THREE MYSTERIOUS CHILDREN

In a conversation with Lucia's aunt, Lucia's mother vented her frustration over her daughter: "These children live some sort of secret life. They are a puzzle to me. When they are alone, they never stop talking, but it's impossible to understand a word they're saying, no matter how carefully you listen. But as soon as someone else appears, they lower their heads and completely clam up. They're a mystery. I can't figure them out."

Note the words "puzzle" and "mystery." Although Lucia's mother was a devout woman, she found it hard to live under one roof with a "visionary" who told stories about having met with, and spoken to, Our Lady. Her credulity and her patience were strained to the limit, and she snapped impatiently: "She's like a worm-eaten wooden saint."

The story of the apparitions is well-known, so we don't need to repeat it in detail here; it will be enough to touch on its main highlights. The more interesting questions for us to ask are What sort of children were Lucia, Jacinta, and Francisco? What kind of life did they lead in the Portuguese countryside? The answers to these questions might help explain how the three children were able to become friends with Our Lady. It might shed some light on why God decided to pour a drop of heaven into the chalice of their simple lives.

According to one account, Jacinta was

> very small and shy. She came up to me slowly. I lifted her up and seated her on a chest. I tell you she's an angel. . . . Wrapped around her head, with the ends tied in back, was a handkerchief. It had a pattern of red branches, and it was a disreputable, tattered old thing. The little jacket she wore wouldn't win any prizes for cleanliness, either. Her dress was reddish, with an extremely wide hem, as is customary in the region. So that's how our little angel was dressed. She has black, charmingly lively eyes. Her whole appearance is extraordinary and you can't take your eyes off of her, though I can't say why this should be the case. She is very timid. After we had chatted for a while, Francisco came in. . . . Jacinta began to show a little more spirit. Not long afterward Lucia came in. You can't imagine Jacinta's happiness on seeing her cousin. Filled with joy, she ran to meet Lucia and wouldn't let go of her for the rest of the interview.

This description of Jacinta is cited from a letter by Doctor Carlos de Azevedo Mendes, in which he shares with his future wife his impressions of the visit he had made on September 7, 1917, to the little village of Aljustrel and to the Cova da Iria, both just a stone's throw from Fatima. Mendes also paints a portrait of Francisco. Though less detailed, the picture is still complete and eloquent: "Francisco came in. He wore a cap pushed back on his head, a very short jacket, a vest worn open over his shirt, and close-fitting pants—in short a grown-up in miniature. He has a wonderful child's face with a lively, mischievous expression. He answers questions with self-assured ease."

That was Francisco: a cheerful, lively, somewhat rough shepherd boy without problems or complexes. In one of the surviving photos of the three children, we see Lucia looking straight ahead; Jacinta stands next to her, a shy wisp of a girl clinging to her cousin for protection; Francisco looks into the camera with a somewhat bolder expression. In the year 1917 the children were, respectively, ten (Lucia), seven (Jacinta), and nine (Francisco). A contemporary account gives us the following description of Lucia: "High, broad forehead. Large, sparkling, chestnut-colored eyes. Thick eyebrows. Flat nose. Large mouth, big lips. Round chin. Face a little broader than normal. Short. Serious and innocent manner. Lively, intelligent, but modest and unassuming. Big, regular hands used to work."

Our Lady predicted a short life for Francisco and Jacinta. Francisco died of the Spanish fever on April 4, 1919. He was just eleven. Jacinta died of pleurisy on February 20, 1920. She was ten. Lucia, by contrast, lived a long life, which crossed the threshold into the third millennium. Lucia's memoirs contain a description of her two cousins, which she wrote at the request of Father Luis Kondor, the vice postulator of the cause for their beatification. Here is what Lucia writes about Jacinta: "Sometimes she was unpleasant to be with because she was so touchy. The slightest question was enough to send her off sulking mulishly in a corner." Concerning Francisco, Lucia says: "He didn't like to dance. He preferred to play the pipe while the other kids danced. He liked to play cards, but he always did his best to lose. If he had lived to adulthood, his main defect would have been an excessively easygoing temperament." He was a "contemplative" child, a "little moralist," who was very creative in making up little sacrifices. We have him to thank for the wording of a prayer that has become a fixed part of the Rosary. At the very end of every decade, we pray: "O my Jesus, forgive us our sins, save us from the fires of hell, lead all souls to heaven, especially those in most need of thy mercy."

The three children often played together. They would throw rocks into the well or see who could win the most buttons. "I was always the one," Sister Lucia recalls, "who ended up losing all the buttons on my clothes." Although Jacinta was small, she was a particularly enthusiastic dancer. So was Lucia. "I would dance on a trunk to the sound of the guitar or the accordion. I would also do a few waltz steps if anyone asked me to. At six the world started to smile on me. Above all, dancing, with everything it represented, was becoming deeply rooted in my poor soul. And I confess that, if our good Lord had not treated me with his special mercy on that point, the devil would have led me to perdition." Lucia's mother, Maria Rosa dos Santos, was the family catechist. In the summer she would teach the children religion while other people were taking their siestas. In wintertime, religion lessons were held in the evening after dinner. The family would sit by the fire roasting chestnuts and sweet acorns. During the corn harvest, the Dos Santos and Martos families would shuck the ears together.

So the children grew up in an atmosphere of peace. They grazed their flocks, played their games, learned the catechism, attended the local parish, and would have fun racing to see who could jump first onto the floats during the Corpus Christi procession. Is it any wonder that even penance should be a game for them (actually, one of their favorite games)? "I knew about the Lord's Passion, but I thought of it as a kind of fable," Sister Lucia candidly confesses.

When we came in from grazing the sheep, we would challenge one another to count the stars, which we called angel lanterns. The adults had recommended that we pray the Rosary after the afternoon snack. Since it always seemed like we had too little time to play, we devised what we thought was a good way of finishing the Rosary in a hurry. We would run our fingers over the beads saying: "Ave Maria, Ave Maria, Ave Maria!" When we'd reached the end of one of the mysteries, we would pause and say the words "Our Father." And so in the twinkling of an eye, as they say, the Rosary was done.

Encounter With the Supernatural

The children's encounter with the supernatural began in the summer of 1915. Lucia saw "as if suspended in the air above the trees a figure that looked like a statue made of ice. It was shining somewhat transparently in the sunlight." The vision recurred the following year. This second time, though, Lucia was tending the flocks with her two small cousins, whereas at the time of the first vision she had been grazing the sheep with two of her friends. The diaphanous figure introduced itself as the "Angel of Portugal, the Angel of Peace." Then Mary appeared for the first time on May 13, 1917, in the guise of "a Lady dressed in white . . . shining as bright as the sun." The children stared openmouthed. "Where are you from?" asked Lucia, who was the only one of the three to pose questions. "From heaven," the Lady replied. "I have come to ask you to return here for the next six months. Always come at the same time on the thirteenth of each month. Then I will tell you who I am and what I wish for. And I will return here a seventh time. . . . Do you wish to offer yourselves to God? Will you bear all the sufferings he will send you in order to make reparation for the sins by which he is offended? Will you pray for the conversion of sinners?" The children were enjoined to silence. But can anyone keep silent about an event that might appear to be incomparably more important than even Jesus's Passion, which until then had seemed like a mere fable to the children? Jacinta was the first one to break the pact. She wept as she was scolded by Lucia.

"All I said was 'What a beautiful Lady.' "

"Now stop crying and don't tell anyone about what the Lady has told us."

"But I already did."

"What did you say?"

"I said that the Lady promised to take us to heaven!"

"Why did you have to go and say *that?*"

"I'm sorry, I'm sorry. I won't say anything to anybody again."

On June 13, the children received the message, which Lucia retained in her prodigious memory and only years later revealed in two distinct stages. The message included a vision of hell and the request to establish devotion to the Immaculate Heart throughout the world, and it also spoke of the conversion of Russia and the attempt to kill the "Bishop dressed in White," the pope.[5]

The Lady told the children about hell. How would they have pictured hell in their minds? "We thought of it as a pit full of animals. People ended up there because they didn't go to confession and because they committed sins. And they stayed there burning forever. 'Those poor, poor people,' we would exclaim in unison. 'Poor sinful souls.' " So the children began fasting for the conversion of sinners. "Two priests advised us to pray for the Holy Father. We didn't know who he was or what Russia was. Jacinta fell so much in love with the Holy Father that whenever she offered her sacrifices to Jesus she would add: 'It's for the Holy Father.' "

On October 13, the Lady revealed her identity: "I am Our Lady of the Rosary. I have come to exhort the faithful to change their lives and to stop offending the Lord by their sins. He is already too much offended. I wish for a chapel in this place. . . . If men amend their ways, the war will soon end."

A huge crowd was present on October 13. The news of the apparitions had spread all over Portugal, and word had it that Our Lady had promised a miraculous sign. At least seventy thousand persons were assembled in the Cova da Iria. Among the throngs of people were photographers and journalists from the Lisbon-based anticlerical newspapers *O Dia* and *O Século*. Then the miracle happened: the sun danced. The phenomenon lasted for several minutes and was visible for miles around. This is how *O Dia* described it:

> [T]he silver-colored sun ... was seen to whirl and wheel about in the circle that had opened up among the clouds. The people all shouted in unison and then fell to their knees on the muddy ground. ... The light took on a beautiful blue tint, as it does when it filters through the stained-glass window of a cathedral, and it spread over the people, who were kneeling with outstretched hands. As the blue color slowly faded, the light seemed to sweep across the yellow grass. ... The people were weeping and praying with uncovered heads in the presence of the miracle for which they had hoped. Each second was so vivid that it seemed like an hour.

The article that appeared in *O Século* was signed by Avelino de Almeida, the chief editor, who had gone to Fatima with the express intention of demolishing what he regarded as a silly superstition, and thus of foiling what he regarded as a Church-organized plot to undo recent developments in Portuguese politics. De Almeida's account offers a wealth of details:

> One could see the huge crowd turning toward the sun, which, standing at the zenith unobstructed by clouds, looked like a piece of opaque silver. One could gaze at it without the least difficulty. It could have been an eclipse, but all of a sudden

there was a great cry, and the nearby spectators started shouting, "A miracle! A miracle!" Before the stupefied eyes of the people, who anxiously peered into the sky with uncovered heads like the multitudes described in the Bible, the sun trembled and darted this way and that. Its brusque movements, which were truly astonishing to behold, defied every known law of astronomy. The sun "danced," as the people typically put it. . . . At that point, the witnesses began to ask one another what they had seen. The overwhelming majority claimed to have seen the sun tremble and dance. Others claimed to have seen the face of the Holy Virgin. Still others swore that the sun had spun on its axis like a giant windmill and that it had plummeted downwards as if to scorch the earth with its rays. A few said that they had seen it change several colors in succession.

Can we say that these articles marked the beginning of Fatima's media career? The answer is probably yes.

Jacinta and Francisco died prematurely, as Heaven prophesied, leaving Lucia behind as the sole witness. By this point, the uproar was in full swing. There was a deafening buzz of criticism, but also a ravenous curiosity among the people. Caravans of devotees came in search of Lucia. But the person officially known as Lucia dos Santos had disappeared. She assumed a new identity, and she was sent abroad for protection. Although she began her schooling with the Dorothean Sisters in Portugal, she eventually continued her studies in Spain (first in Túy, then in Pontevedra). Finally, she became a Dorothean herself. It was not until 1948 that she managed to obtain Pope Pius XII's permission to become a Carmelite nun in the convent of Santa Teresa in Coimbra, Portugal.

At this point, the next-to-last character in our story entered the scene: Sister Maria Celina of Jesus Crucified, the prioress of Sister Lucia's convent. "They tried," Maria Celina wrote, to turn her into a city girl. She was handed over to the care of a proper lady, who was to educate her and teach her correct manners, which were quite foreign to her habitual behavior. One day, when she was thirteen, they made her put on a corset that was so tight that it restricted her breathing. She stole back to her room and put on the peasant costume she had brought with her from Fatima. She returned to the table to the great surprise of the lady, the bishop, and a canon. "Miss, what have you done?" The immediate answer: "I'm sorry, but I couldn't eat with that corset on. The only thing I've ever seen that was tighter was the saddle on my mom's donkey." This was met by general laughter.

Lucia lived a normal Carmelite's life. She was always faithful to the motto "Outside like everyone else, inside like no one else." She served as bookkeeper, sacristan, and gardener. The rest of her day was taken up with writing. In mid-2004 her health deteriorated. "No one wants to die, but it's very hard being old! Our Lady said that I would remain for a while . . . but look at how much time has passed already!" She was kept constantly informed about the progress of John Paul II's illness. Her cell contained a little statue of Our Lady of Fatima, a gift from John Paul II. The rosary she held was also a gift from the pope, one he had sent her for her birthday. On February 13, 2005, she opened her eyes, looked for a moment at her sisters and the crucifix, and then closed them forever. She was ninety-seven. Her last words were: "I offer this suffering for the Holy Father."

NOT YOUR ORDINARY RED HAT

I am in the archbishop's palace in Genoa. One of the ushers, wheezing slightly, says to me: "We finally get a simple and down-to-earth cardinal, but just when we start becoming used to him, the Holy Father up and takes him away." Archbishop Bertone is holding an open house (which is only one of several, in fact). Those who like to exaggerate the inaccessibility of cardinals should take note. I have had a certain modest experience of red hats in my time, but this one stands out.

In June 2006, Benedict XVI appointed Cardinal Tarcisio Bertone as his secretary of state. Benedict's number one collaborator is a member of the Salesian order, a man at once calm and effervescent, prudent and unafraid to act. Bertone strikes me as totally different from the dull ecclesiastical bureaucrats you sometimes see portrayed on television. He is anything but the spoiled viceroy of a remote sovereign, anything but out of touch with the real life of the men and women entrusted to his care. He stands in a big room in the archbishop's residence, patiently receiving members of the faithful who, though unknown to him personally, come to bid him farewell and offer him their best wishes for his new task. He greets them "Genoese style," which is to say affectionately, but unsentimentally. He prays with his visitors, shakes their hands, and pats them on the back. His way of treating people reinforces my conviction that it's not impossible to attain perfection even at the top of the Church organization.

It is a sultry, late July morning. "Your Eminence," I say when my turn comes, "either we take advantage of these last few days when you can still come and go freely, or else we'll have to abandon our project." The cardinal calls his secretary: "When am I supposed to go to Torriglia?" "At the beginning of August," Don Stefano replies. The cardinal turns to me and says: "Okay, come visit me in Torriglia and we'll have a working vacation."

And so, brandishing a tape recorder and armed with several sheets of paper crammed with questions, I find myself in Torriglia, which is located in the Genoese Apennines, about 2,600 feet above sea level. I am enjoying the tranquility of a retreat house run by an order of nuns known as the Suore Brignoline, or Brignoline Sisters. In addition to myself, the company includes Cardinal Bertone, Lucia (is this a coincidence or what?) Gradi, the cardinal's "undersecretary," and thirteen nuns (*thir-teen:* another amazing coincidence). Lucia has the thankless task of shuttling between Torriglia and the archbishop's palace to fish letters, documents, notes, or photos out of mountainous piles of boxes waiting to be shipped to the Vatican.

Why did one of the highest-ranking officials of the Congregation for the Doctrine of the Faith feel the need to rush to Coimbra to meet with an old Carmelite nun surrounded by an aura of mystery and sanctity? Has everything pertaining to the Third Secret been said and revealed? And what is the cardinal's general assessment of Marian shrines and the faith that pilgrims to these sanctuaries so defiantly wear on their sleeves? And, most important, who was Sister Lucia? Was she a credible witness, or was she a visionary dreamer, or even the accomplice of some sinister plot? Was she, like Jacinta and Francisco before her, the last victim of a rather ordinary mental delusion?

What began as an interview about the Secret of Fatima turned out to be something more: a reflection on faith in the contemporary world and an exploration of the surprising twists in the story of John Paul II's pontificate, to which Fatima provides one of the most dramatic and spectacular interpretive keys. The interview became an effort to piece together an extraordinary jigsaw puzzle, a mosaic, whose elements are as subtle as the boundary between everyday life and mystery, between the visible and the unseen.

Perhaps the fluid nature of this boundary explains why crowds of pilgrims still flock to the Marian shrines. For the shrines offer a space in which visitors can rediscover the warmth of encounter with God, and can recover the tangible, concrete experience of the divine that is the hallmark of the Gospel. The shrines offer a rich feast of popular piety to undernourished souls who cannot feed on the cold, dry liturgies invented by the theorists, the specialists in the things of God (which not all of them truly are). For its part, Fatima speaks not just to the mind, but also to the body. At Fatima the pilgrims sing, participate in processions, cross the square on their knees, shed tears, implore favors, write messages and toss them at the feet of the Virgin. They light candles, send postcards, and buy scapulars and little bottles of blessed water. "The heart has reasons of which reason is unaware," Pascal once said. Fatima helps us rediscover the reasons of the heart, the physical side of religion. It presents us with the reasons to believe, without eliminating the possibility of finding reasons to doubt. For Fatima brings us into contact with our God who, through Mary, wants to be a gift, not a diktat. God's vengeance is his love for us, as Pope Benedict XVI explained during his 2006 visit to Bavaria.

Cardinal Bertone did not evade the questions I asked him. Rather, he took every question to heart and he dug into his memory and his notes to answer it. "The demons and souls . . . like transparent burning embers; . . . war . . . and persecutions of the Church; . . . Penance, penance, penance! And we saw in an immense light that is God."[6] These citations from the Secret suggest what a strange and unusual journey in the footsteps of God this book has turned out to be. For the cardinal and me, the journey began in hell, but, almost without realizing it, we ended up in paradise.

PART ONE

PARSING

THE

PROPHECY

OF

FATIMA:

—— AN INTERVIEW WITH ——
CARDINAL TARCISIO BERTONE

A RADIANT, CREDIBLE WITNESS

Cardinal Bertone, in your capacity as papal legate, you enjoyed more regular contact than any other person with Sister Maria Lucia De Jesus e Do Coração Imaculado in her convent in Coimbra, Portugal. You met with her between 2000 and 2003, first in your capacity as secretary of the Congregation for the Doctrine of the Faith, where you worked under Cardinal Joseph Ratzinger, and then during your tenure as archbishop of Genoa. Some of the meetings were of an official nature, and were followed by either press conferences or media reports. Others were of a more private character. Finally, after Lucia died at the age of ninety-seven on February 13, 2005, you presided at her solemn funeral Mass.

There were three meetings that you might label "official." The first one took place on April 27, 2000, just a few days before Pope John Paul II's pilgrimage to Fatima, where he was planning to beatify Lucia's two cousins, Jacinta and Francisco. The pope had decided to reveal the third part of the so-called Secret of Fatima, and he needed a definitive interpretation from Lucia. Then I went back to Coimbra on November 17, 2000. At this point, the Secret had already been revealed. The reason for my second trip was the hue and cry raised in the media about the supposed *omissis,* the parts that had allegedly been left out of the text released by the Vatican. I wanted a confirmation that the Fatima message had been completely revealed, and that Sister Lucia didn't have any more notes about the Third Secret pertaining to, say, Pope John Paul I. The third trip was on December 9, 2003, according to the official appointment calendar I kept as Archbishop of Genoa.

So there were three official meetings. How long did they last altogether?

At least ten hours. I met with Lucia personally on other occasions, but it was always during short stops in Coimbra to celebrate Mass. After the liturgy, we would exchange short greetings, but these brief meetings had absolutely no official significance or relevance to the Church.

How did the official visits come about? The first one, in particular, was preceded by a letter from Pope John Paul II. "Sister Maria Lucia," he wrote, "you may speak openly and candidly to Archbishop Bertone, who will report your answers directly to me."[1] What a calling card! How willing did you find Sister Lucia?

Our meetings were very cordial. Of course, given the wishes of the pope, Sister Lucia was ready to confide in me and, I would say, to talk about the genuineness of her recollection and description of the events in which she had played a part.

What sort of impression did this very punctilious, very persistent woman make on you? After all, for the first time in decades she was experiencing the joy of being listened to by a pope.

What was striking from my point of view was how fresh her memory was, how trenchant her images were, how precise she was. When she recounted events, she would paint a sequence of images so vivid that you thought you were watching a movie. She was a "good Samaritan" of the memory. I immediately sensed her radiant awareness of having received a very definite mission. She was humble and obedient, but—as you just said—she was also persistently determined to give a full explanation of the messages that Our Lady had entrusted to her. As she was speaking, I thought: "Here is a woman who never lets any difficulty stop her." She had suffered, she had struggled, and now she was overcoming the last resistance and persuading the world. After having stored in her heart the events in which she had participated and the message she had received, she relived and reread both with a lucidity and a calm that only enhanced her credibility. She was a witness in the fullest sense of the word. Are my remarks pertinent?

I would say that they're fundamentally important, Your Eminence. Who is better qualified than you to describe what sort of person Lucia was? Millions of people have looked up, and still look up, to Sister Lucia. She is a mediator, a bridge, a messenger, an eyewitness. If Lucia is credible, then Fatima has a much more serious claim on our attention, and believers can be more confident that its mystery does not reflect darkness, but the light of God's glory.

I noticed in our conversations that Sister Lucia was able to formulate the heart of the message in a simple, clear fashion. I also noticed that she would cite the Virgin's exhortation (from the October 13 apparition) as a kind of basic reference point: "I have come to exhort the faithful to change their lives and to stop offending the Lord by their sins. He is already too much offended." Lucia found guidance in her prayerful reading of Scripture, and her inspiration flowed from an interior listening to the Word of God. She gave people the courage to convert. She also presented a substantive vision of the nature and goals of the Christian life, a vision whose clarity strengthened people's resolve to continue believing and living moral lives. She had thought things through and had reached a deep level of settled conviction. She was persistent, stubborn, and exuberant. Such qualities are not at all in conflict with the ABCs of Christian behavior. On the contrary, if they're properly channeled, they are very useful antidotes to anxiety, uncertainty, and doubt about one's earthly and eternal destiny.

How about her memory? Was it particularly accurate?

Her memory was absolutely accurate.

Were you alone during the first conversation?

No. The first time I was accompanied by the bishop of Leiria-Fatima, Serafin de Sousa Ferreira e Silva, who helped me with the languages. We spoke a bit of Spanish and a bit of Portuguese. I'm not tremendous in either language, but the conversation was perfectly comprehensible. Anyway, I also needed a witness who could vouch for the precise meaning of Lucia's statements, as well as of her questions to me and my replies to them. The pope's letter cleared away every hesitation from Lucia's mind. She said: "Okay, I will tell you everything you ask."

I imagine that she was very happy.

Yes she was. Don't forget that she had written several letters to John Paul II's predecessors.

And did they answer her?

I don't think so. Correction: at least not *officially*. They may have responded through intermediaries, but I have never looked into it. What I do know is that in the last long letter she sent to John Paul II, Sister Lucia asked for three things. I don't know, though, whether this letter is confidential or whether it is under lock and key in the CDF archives.

Seeing as how you are piquing our curiosity here, perhaps you could give us some hints about the contents of the letter.

First off, Lucia requested the beatification of the two *pastorinhos,* Jacinta and Francisco. There was a certain resistance to proceeding with the beatification. Some argued that, if we beatified Sister Lucia's cousins, it would be like beatifying Lucia *ante mortem,* before her death, as well. The counterargument that finally prevailed was that each person is judged on his own virtues according to the standard procedures stipulated by the Holy See. We don't make judgments about the holiness of a group, but decide who is a saint on a person-by-person basis. Now, as we all know, the two shepherd children were judged worthy of beatification because of their heroic virtue and their self-sacrifice for the Church and the conversion of sinners.

Can we say, though, that Sister Lucia's testimony played a decisive role in getting them elevated to the glories of the altar?

I can't deny that. The testimony of relatives, priests who knew them, and the bishop was also important. Don't forget the basic requirement, either. God had to give his seal of approval by granting a miracle through the intercession of the two *pastorinhos*, and the miracle had to be recognized as such by the Congregation for the Causes of Saints.

THE ROSARY AND THE LITURGY

Jacinta and Francisco are the youngest non-martyrs ever to be beatified in the history of the Church. At the time of the apparitions, Lucia was ten, Jacinta Marto was seven, and Jacinta's brother Francisco was nine. The miracle you mentioned just now is very rare in that it was performed by two saints at once. Maria Emilia Santos, who had been paralyzed for twenty-three years with tuberculosis of the bone, was healed by the intercession of the two children. The story of this healing made a big impression on me when I heard it in Fatima while covering the beatification of Francisco and Jacinta on May 13, 2000, for Italian TV.

And what was Sister Lucia's second request?

She asked that the pope proclaim the Rosary as a liturgical prayer. Sister Lucia would light up when she prayed the Rosary. She recited it with the pope during the Jubilee of the Bishops. Though she was in Coimbra, she was beamed live into Saint Peter's Square. They had also placed a statue of Our Lady of Fatima before the portico of the basilica.

Did she give any reasons for her request?

I would say so. We begin the Rosary with an invocation of the Most Holy Trinity. We then immerse ourselves in the mysteries of Revelation, which culminate in Our Lady's transformation into a living temple of the Holy Spirit. As Sister Lucia pointed out, the prayers that make up the Rosary are all biblical ones inspired and taught by God himself. The Gloria was sung by the angels at Jesus's birth. The Ave Maria begins with the words of greeting that the angel Gabriel addressed to Mary at the Annunciation. After this opening, the Hail Mary goes on to cite Elizabeth's greeting to her cousin Mary that we find recorded in Luke's Gospel: "Blessed art thou among women, and blessed is the fruit of thy womb" (Lk 1:42). This puts me in mind of something Sister Lucia once said: "The Rosary is the most beautiful prayer Heaven has taught us. More than any other prayer, it leads us to a better knowledge of God and his redemptive work."

Plus, if I am not mistaken, Mary recommended the Rosary as a weapon of peace.

"Pray the Rosary every day to obtain peace in the world and the end of war." According to Sister Lucia's account, the heavenly Lady was very explicit about this. "Our Lady," Lucia wrote,

> did not predict that we would have pleasures, earthly joys, honor, power, or material goods. Nor did she predict that we would become big, important people in this world, which is nothing but illusion, blindness, and vanity, and where every goal is sought with so much anguish, deceit, and injustice. "Do you wish to offer yourselves to God? Will you bear all the sufferings he will send you in order to make reparation for the sins by which he is offended? Will you pray for the conversion of sinners?" "Yes, we will."

"It was with full awareness of this prediction of many sufferings," Sister Lucia remarked, "that I pronounced my 'Yes.' And the Lord did not let us down, nor was his grace ever lacking, as Our Lady had promised: 'The grace of God will be your strength.' "

In spite of that, Sister Lucia's request was liturgically incorrect.

I only said that her request was well-argued. But that doesn't mean that it would persuade liturgists. The Rosary is a compendium of the New Testament, but . . .

But?

There's a pretty high standard for what counts as liturgical prayer.

The Rosary is a staple of popular devotion, rather than a liturgical prayer.

It's a form of devotion. It inspired John Paul II to write a wonderful apostolic letter, *Rosarium Virginis Mariae,* which encouraged the practice of the Rosary among the world's Catholics.

John Paul II went on to proclaim the Year of the Rosary. He also enriched the Rosary with an additional set of mysteries, the so-called Mysteries of Light, an addition that reinforced the Rosary's biblical character. Plus, the 104th and last apostolic journey of the "totus tuus" Pope outside Italy was to the Marian shrine of Lourdes in August 2004.

The Year of the Rosary and the introduction of the Luminous Mysteries were exactly the right answers to Lucia's request. She herself was overjoyed.

Her third request had to do with the publication of her book *Calls from the Message of Fatima,* which in the meantime has appeared in several languages. It's a little-known fact that people from all over the world would write to Sister Lucia in the Carmel of Saint Teresa in Coimbra. She spent her life writing. She had a distinctive style of handwriting; it was compact, without erasures or flourishes, and as precise as if it were a mirror image of her soul. As a child she was illiterate. It was only as a teenager that she learned to write. She said that she would be very happy if the Holy Father would give her permission to publish *Calls from the Message of Fatima,* which basically consists of the answers to the letters she had received. You see, she had never received permission to publish her book.

Why on earth not?

The thinking was "If we let Sister Lucia publish a book, it will immediately become a best seller, and everyone will regard the author as some kind of saint." I took up Sister Lucia's request with Cardinal Ratzinger and then with the pope. I said: "But Holy Father, there are so many books of theology and pseudo-theology in circulation today; a book by Sister Lucia can only do good. If need be, we'll have it revised." The pope granted his permission. A Carmelite professor of spiritual theology, the late Father Jesús Castellano, read through the manuscript, but he didn't make any major corrections. There was no substantial editing that might have seriously affected the book's content. Some critics have claimed that the book was significantly modified, but they are wrong. There was no need for corrections or censorship. One of the main ideas of Sister Lucia's book (which, I should add, she presents in a very sober fashion) is that the Church ought to acknowledge Mary as the "Co-redemptrix" of humanity.

That is not a new idea. It is defended by a few theologians, not to mention by the members of an American movement associated with an organization called the Fatima Center, which publishes a magazine entitled The Fatima Crusader.

Both the Congregation for the Doctrine of the Faith and the Pontifical International Marian Academy had already raised some critical points about the idea of "co-redemption." They were especially concerned about its impact on ecumenism. Nevertheless, Sister Lucia's book is very worthwhile. It is the theological distillation of a lifetime of intense meditation on the mysteries of the Christian faith. Even the bishop of Leiria-Fatima, who was initially reluctant to back the publication, eventually agreed to be involved in the project. In fact, he ended up writing the preface.

Cardinal Bertone, let's go back to April 27, 2000. Had you prepared questions and did you have a notebook or a tape recorder?

Well, I didn't bring any tape recorder, but I did take notes, which then served as the basis for a summary of the conversation published by the Congregation for the Doctrine of the Faith. The questions revolved mainly around the genuineness of the text of the third part of the Secret of Fatima.

Which text do you mean?

The one kept in the secret archives of the former Holy Office. These archives contain all the material regarding the Fatima apparitions, including Sister Lucia's memoirs, her other manuscripts, and the famous open envelope—whose contents had already been read by three popes.

You mean John XXIII, Paul VI, and John Paul II?

That much is certain. I say "three" because I still believe that, despite being nicknamed the Pope of Fatima, Pius XII never actually learned the contents of the third part of the Secret. I base my case for this on the reconstruction of the history of the envelope. The Third Secret was taken to the Vatican's Secret Archives in 1957 by the nuncio, Archbishop Fernando Cento. The transferal of the Secret thus occurs pretty much at the end of Pope Eugenio Pacelli's life. Moreover, there's no record of anything like a request for, or transfer or reception of, the envelope, or of a private audience that might have dealt with it. In short, the text was not taken to the papal apartments or to the secretariat of state.

There were actually two envelopes.

Yes. One envelope was marked "Third Part of the Secret," and it contained a second envelope, marked "1960," which originated from Sister Lucia herself. We can come back to this particular point later. The second envelope contained four pages in Sister Lucia's hand. I showed her these pages. Obviously, her vision was failing. So I let her physically touch her letter, turn it over in her hands, examine it, and take time to identify it and put it into focus. Those were long, suspenseful moments, and we sat there looking at each other wondering what would happen.

Then Sister Lucia exclaimed: "Yes, yes, these are my sheets and my envelope; these are the sheets I used and this is my writing. This is my envelope, this is my writing, this is my text."

So there was no preset battery of questions. But the meeting with Sister Lucia was crucial. I assume that you planned it with the pope and Cardinal Ratzinger. Did you consult any Mariologists?

No, we didn't consult any Mariologists. We had a meeting with the Holy Father. It was attended by Cardinal Ratzinger, Cardinal Sodano, and the substitute secretary of state, Giovanni Battista Cardinal Re, as well as the pope's personal secretary, Stanislaw Dziwisz.

Who decided to publish the Secret?

The pope himself. During the meeting I just mentioned, the decision was made to send me to Coimbra to interview Sister Lucia. The two main issues were the genuineness of the document in the possession of the Congregation for the Doctrine of the Faith and the authentic interpretation of this document. I more or less arranged the questions in my mind, but, just to be sure, I made a written list. Obviously, before leaving I consulted with Cardinal Ratzinger during an internal meeting of the Congregation. He mentioned that he would provide a theological interpretation of the Secret, which he later did in writing.

Was it the first time you had read the document?

Yes.

Was Cardinal Ratzinger already familiar with it?

He was.

And what sort of effect did it have on you? What was your immediate reaction? What first went through your mind? The fact is, you were part of a handful of privileged souls whom the rest of the world envied. You got to see the veil lifted from the secret of the century.

I compare it to what you experience when you have a confused intuition of something that suddenly snaps into clear, sharp focus. It was like seeing a kaleidoscope of images come together. Sometimes when you first look at an abstract painting you feel lost, because its meaning is a bit cryptic. Then you read the title, and it gives you a clue to interpreting what you see. When I read the few lines containing the Secret, I immediately saw a connection with a whole sequence of events, words, speeches, and statements of John Paul II. My first thought was that the text referred to the mystery of the attempt on the pope's life. There were a lot of signs in the twentieth century, but no one would have predicted gunshots in Saint Peter's Square, not to mention the details uncovered by the police investigation. It would have sounded too much like some apocalyptic prophecy. A professional killer tries to assassinate the pope in Saint Peter's Square, which is the home, not only of the pontiff himself, but of the whole world as well. The shooting of John Paul II was an unprecedented event.

THE TRANSFORMING POWER OF FATIMA

Pope John Paul often resorted to solemn and dramatic language when he spoke of the attempt on his life. The shooting happened on May 13, 1981, the anniversary of Mary's first appearance to the three shepherd children of Fatima. I've read that Albert Cardinal Decourtray worriedly informed John Paul II of then current rumors to the effect that a prophecy of Nostradamus would be fulfilled during the pope's upcoming apostolic journey to Lyons, France, which was scheduled for a supposedly unlucky time (October 1986). John Paul II swept aside the cardinal's concerns with a smile and an ironic comment: "I assure you, Your Eminence, that no place is as dangerous as Saint Peter's Square."

When I read the Third Secret, it was immediately obvious to me that it referred to the assassination attempt. I knew that it applied to the contemporary Church and to its pope. It was like a photograph that vividly portrayed the great martyrdom of the Church in the twentieth century. Remember, the text describes a huge procession of martyrs, a "city half in ruins," the Bishop's "halting step," and his "pain and sorrow" over "the souls of the corpses he met on his way."[1]

It's a very powerful description, no doubt. It reminds one of certain passages in the Book of Revelation. And of other things as well. For example, it puts me in mind of a dialogue that took place in the country church that we attended when I was growing up. During the Forty Hours devotion, which has since fallen into disuse, two preachers bantered back and forth about hell, paradise, purgatory, and the blood shed by multitudes of good Christians in defense of their faith. I was a child at the time, but I remember that the congregation listened breathlessly in rapt attention to this dramatization of the titanic battle between good and evil. We were actors in a sacred play of the sort depicted in the splendid frescoes of medieval churches. This is just one example of what was once a ubiquitous, and singularly effective, form of popular catechesis.

Right, but the description in the Third Secret was more concise. It wasn't the sort of newspaper account or TV report we would tend to imagine today. Rather, it was a vision, a prophetic vision. In a single picture, a single narrative recounted in the present tense, it captured an event that actually unfolded over time. Moreover, this event was one that involved the pope, bishops, priests, men and women religious, and, as the text of the Secret puts it, "various laypeople of different ranks and positions."[2]

At the time of your first meeting with her, Sister Lucia was ninety-three. She was old, but she was still persistent, courageous, and even stubborn. Her memoirs reveal her personal style. I know I'm making commonplace psychological observations, but I am encouraged to make them by a (to me) surprising section of Cardinal Ratzinger's "Theological Commentary" on the Third Secret, where the cardinal discusses what he calls the "anthropological structure of private revelations." When I was studying philosophy and theology, I always tried to keep in mind an adage of the medieval philosophers (which I first heard as a student at the Catholic University of Milan in a lecture by Professor Sofia Vanni Rovighi): Quidquid recipitur, ad modum recipientis recipitur. *In translation, this sentence means: Whatever is received, is received according to the condition of the one who receives it. At Fatima, three children were profoundly touched by the supernatural. Since they were children at the time, it's not unreasonable to think that God could speak through them using language that was rich in images.*

Similarly, since Lucia, unlike the other two visionaries, outlived childhood, it's logical to suppose that her understanding of the revelation would have been a kind of work in progress. It wouldn't be surprising if she had continued to decode the message as the years went by, or if she had experienced God's revelation of it as a dynamic process that gradually transformed her entire existence.

Personally, I don't believe that it was only the Secret that changed Sister Lucia. No, she was transformed by the revelations of Fatima taken as a whole. The cause of the change was her direct experience of the divine. Seeing Our Lady, meeting her, talking with her—all of these events shaped Lucia when she was a child. The Secret is just the tip of the iceberg. The real center lies in all the revelations taken as a whole. The visions actually start quite early. In her posthumously published book *Come vedo il Messaggio di Fatima*, Sister Lucia nicely conveys the way in which the children became more and more clearly aware that something extraordinary was happening. It all started with the vision of the angels: First it was the guardian angel, then the "Angel of Peace." This was in 1916.

> God began the preparation of the instruments he had chosen while they prayed and played without a care in the world. He did this by making an object pass slowly and gently in front of them. It was similar to a snow white cloud, and it was more brilliant than the sun, but it had a human form. It seemed to detach itself from the sky and to descend toward them. It drew their gaze and caught their attention. "What is that?" the poor children asked one another. "I don't know." Even today I don't know with certainty. But what happened afterward led me to believe that it was our guardian angel who, without clearly showing himself, was preparing us for the fulfillment of God's plans.

The angel opens a doorway into infinity for Lucia. She begins to take a step beyond the physical. This act of transcendence gradually permeates and takes over her entire life, and the transformation continues on through the time of the revelation of the Third Secret. If we apply the classical scholastic axiom you quoted just now about the *quidquid recipitur,* I don't know to what extent the shepherd children actually did receive the message. Jacinta and Francisco got only fragments of it. It was Lucia who received and committed to memory the whole wealth and drama of the Fatima message.

It was Lucia, in fact, who explained things to her young cousins. Jacinta and Francisco heard and saw what was going on, but they didn't understand it.

Lucia was the one whose job was to communicate. I couldn't tell you what she did and didn't explain. I didn't ask any specific questions about that. But Lucia was the one who kept the Secret, especially the third part, her whole life long.

What effect did the apparitions have on Lucia? When you met her, she was already advanced in years. But something of her experience of the divine, of the "heavenly grammar" she had learned from Our Lady, must have remained in her soul.

The apparitions were always in the background. When Sister Lucia did explicitly touch on them, I caught a glimpse of her inner joy, which enabled her to communicate the same joy and peace to others. Depending on what the Lady had commanded her, she would either speak, relating what she knew, or else she would remain silent. For years, Lucia was a woman of silence. Bodily infirmity also obliged her to remain silent, but her silence gave her a certain—how shall I put it?—expansive agility. Whereas a lot of mystics experience a sort of annihilation in the divine presence, Lucia exulted with joy; rather than finding it hard to speak, she was actually something of an enthusiastic communicator. A supernatural sign would tell her when to be silent, especially when she was asked tricky questions about the Secret. She had an interior censor, and she could get herself out of a jam with a simple glance. "During the interrogations," Sister Lucia writes,

> I felt an inward inspiration prompting me to give answers that, while not untruthful, managed to avoid revealing what I was supposed to be concealing at the time. On this score, I still have just one doubt: Wouldn't it have been better to divulge everything during the canonical inquest? I am not troubled by scruples over having kept silence, because at the time I myself was unaware of the importance of the inquest. I did think it was odd that they should order me to swear to tell the truth. I had no problem doing that. I had no idea at the time that the devil would later take advantage of this oath to torment me with endless scruples. But that is all over now, thank God.

The Italian philosopher Massimo Cacciari's immediate objection was: Why didn't Lucia write things down earlier? It's obvious that, as she looked back on the events in retrospect, her memory would be conditioned by the books she had read and the homilies she had listened to. So many filters, so many outside influences! But it's not up to me to respond to Cacciari. Umberto Eco, after raising the same objection as Cacciari, goes on to opine that "the inconographic tradition," especially depictions of the Book of Revelation, "influenced Sister Lucia's memory." "An allegory is not a prophecy to be taken literally. . . . Let's put what we have said in more secular terms: If there are no Jungian archetypes, then every visionary sees what his culture has taught him to see." So, Your Eminence, you see how easy it is to get caught up in a tangled skein of interpretations. In my humble opinion, if we were looking for an—admittedly very distant—point of comparison, we could say that the Evangelists also wrote several years after Jesus's death and Resurrection. Plus, even Jesus's Resurrection is described in the New Testament as an "apparition."

That's a good point. In Jesus's time, the events were first transmitted orally, then recorded in a written narrative. It was only when she was about twenty that Sister Lucia started to get the hang of reading and writing. Mary had ordered her to keep in her heart what she had seen. It was José Correia da Silva (1872–1957), the first bishop of Leiria-Fatima, who convinced her to write. She started with thirty-eight sheets of paper, which she covered on both sides with her vigorous, neat handwriting. There are no erasures. The bishop had requested information concerning Jacinta and Francisco. He was hoping for testimony that would help to advance the cause of their beatification, which had recently been opened. "Despite the repugnance I feel, I will obey," was Lucia's laconic response. She added this remark: "Although I willingly obey you, I hope, Your Excellency, that you will allow me to keep to myself certain things that, because they refer to my person, I would prefer be read only on the threshold of eternity." The bishop insisted, however, and even these last lines of defense eventually fell. Sister Lucia was a nun, a Carmelite, and she was used to discretion and obedience. Her lack of education as a child was like a permanent scar on her soul. She often complained that she felt uncertain when it came to dates. Neither she nor her cousins (they even less so, in fact) could count the days of the week, the months, and the years. She makes up for the lacunae in her recollection of dates with the realism of her narrative and her focus on the essentials of the story. So there is nothing surprising in the fact that Sister Lucia wrote at a considerable distance from the events. It seems to have escaped Cacciari that Lucia never wrote anything on her own initiative or by her own decision. She wrote because she was commanded to.

Speaking of dates, the first two parts of the Secret were written down in the memoir of August 31, 1941. Sister Lucia then added some annotations on

December 8 of the same year. The third part was written in Túy, Spain, on January 3, 1944. Excuse the question, but did you put Sister Lucia under oath at the beginning of your April 27, 2000, meeting?

No. I didn't ask her to swear to anything. It seemed unnecessary, not to mention subtly offensive and coercive. I asked: "Is this the only text you wrote?" She replied: "Yes, this is it." I was sitting across from a woman filled with the calm determination of a person with a mission to accomplish, a mission she had been asked to give her whole life to bear witness to. A woman like that didn't need to be put under oath. I had absolutely no doubts about her sincerity, just as I didn't have any doubts about the sincerity of her prioress in Coimbra, Sister Maria Celina of Jesus Crucified, who wrote a moving recollection of Lucia Rosa dos Santos after her death.

The end-of-the-millennium Jubilee was already chock-full of religious events. Why was it necessary to throw in the publication of the Third Secret on top of everything else?

It was John Paul II who made that decision. One of the many events that took place that year was the beatification of the *pastorinhos* of Fatima. If we had gone ahead with the beatification of Jacinta and Francisco without saying anything about the Third Secret, our decision would have been interpreted as an inexplicable and unforgivable omission. It would have unleashed an endless flood of speculation. The Fatimists were already doing a full court press, and we didn't want to give them a pretext. There are legions of people itching for apocalypse, and we didn't want to give them any ammunition, or provide an outlet for their totally absurd theories. As pastors, we were eager to defuse the issue.

Who argued for the pastoral opportuneness of forestalling international public opinion with an act of full disclosure?

I think the pope made the argument at the end of a consultation with his advisors.

Is it your opinion that John Paul II had already read the text of the Third Secret before it was brought to him as he lay in a hospital bed at the Gemelli Clinic in July 1981?

I'm convinced that he hadn't read it.

Are you convinced or are you certain?

I'm certain. I'm going by the documentation in the archives of the CDF, which I compared with records in the archives of the secretariat of state.

JOHN PAUL II: THE POPE OF
THE THIRD SECRET

John Paul II was a pope whose devotion to Mary was inscribed in the very core of his being. So, if he was aware of the existence of the Third Secret, why didn't he choose to read it as soon as he was elected to the papacy?

Your inference doesn't follow, in my opinion. You're forgetting the role played by the pope's personal sensibility and his particular circumstances. On being elected pope, John Paul II set out to re-evangelize the world. The shooting was a sign written in blood, and it injected a new level of depth into his already immense popular appeal. The effects of the assassination attempt on the man Karol Wojtyla remain unfathomable. Surely the blood he shed was a sign that moved him to dedicate himself totally to his mission, even to the point of ignoring the calculations of human prudence, including the basic, instinctive consideration of physical safety. After the assassination attempt, the world suddenly discovered that there was a mystery in Karol Wojtyla. The world found itself face-to-face with a life that crossed the boundary into the realm of the absolute. When John Paul II read the Secret on the ninth floor of the Gemelli Clinic, it had the force of a revelation for him. By contrast, it had a much lighter impact, if you will, when it passed through the hands of John XXIII, who read the text, paused for a moment of reflection, and then said, "Okay, we'll just let it rest here." John XXIII, who had just called the Second Vatican Council, wasn't particularly touched by the manuscript. He left it to his successors to take any further decisions regarding its fate.

And yet John Paul II, in an address he gave in November 1980 in Fulda, Germany, tried to temper excessive curiosity about Sister Lucia's text, which at the time had not yet been published. "We have to be ready for impending tribulations, which may require the sacrifice of our lives and the gift of ourselves to and for Christ. The intensity of these trials," the pope added, "can be diminished by your and our prayer, but they cannot be avoided, because it is only through trials that true renewal can come. Let us be strong and let us make ready, trusting in Christ and his Mother." These words are enough to make you shudder. "Let us make ready": The pope was ready for what would be his most painful trial.

There's no reason to suppose that Cardinal Ratzinger thought John Paul II's words in Fulda indicated any knowledge of the Third Secret on the pontiff's part. There's no difficulty in assuming that John Paul II delivered the lines you cited without having read Lucia's text. He was simply taking stock of the general situation of the Church and reviewing the problems existing at that particular point in time. The basic question was: Who were the intended recipients of the Fatima texts? Was it the whole Church? Well, in the first place the texts were intended for the popes, and it was the popes who had the personal (and final) authority to decide how to use them. Pope John XXIII wasn't particularly disturbed by the Third Secret, and he sent it back to the Holy Office. Paul VI, who was a man of great intelligence and deep spirituality, read it on March 27, 1965, but decided not to publish it. These two popes probably consulted with their respective prefects of the CDF, who, going by what happened, were not favorably disposed toward its publication. The assassination attempt put everything in a new light. "If I am not dead, it is thanks to God's mercy," John Paul II said in Todi, Italy. What he means by "God's mercy" includes Mary's infinite tenderness. While still in the Gemelli Clinic, the pope wrote: "It was a mother's hand that guided the bullet's path and in his throes the pope halted at the threshold of death."[1] Wojtyla's Marian piety becomes Christocentric. It becomes the very suffering of Christ on the cross.

The first and second parts of the Secret bring before our minds terrifying visions of hell, devotion to the Immaculate Heart of Mary, the Second World War, and the need for Russia to convert lest it spread its errors and thereby fan the flames of war and persecution. "The good will be martyred; the Holy Father will have much to suffer; various nations will be annihilated."[2] It's a fact that in 1917 no one could have imagined such things coming to pass. The three shepherd children were unaware of the larger world. They had never even heard of Russia. They were so puzzled by that unknown name that, as they talked it over one day, Francisco said: "Do you think she means Uncle Jaquim's donkey?" (The donkey happened to be called "Russa".) At this point, Lucia replied knowingly: "I think it must be some very Catholic lady." The third part of the Secret begins with a call to penance. It then goes on to describe a "Bishop dressed in White" who falls at the foot of a big cross, shot dead by a group of soldiers firing at him repeatedly with guns and arrows. And then two angels appear holding a crystal aspersorium, in which they gather the blood of the martyrs and pour it out on the souls who come close to God.

Let me start by pointing out that Sister Lucia herself provides a key to interpreting the third part of the Secret in a letter she wrote to the Holy Father on May 12, 1982, where she says the following:

> The third part of the Secret refers to Our Lady's words: "If not [Russia] will spread her errors throughout the world, causing wars and persecutions of the Church. The good will be martyred; the Holy Father will have much to suffer; various nations will be annihilated" (13-VII-1917). The third part of the secret is a symbolic revelation, referring to this part of the Message, conditioned by whether we accept or not what the

Message itself asks of us: "If my requests are heeded, Russia will be converted, and there will be peace; if not, she will spread her errors throughout the world, etc. . . . Since we did not heed this appeal of the Message, we see that it has been fulfilled, Russia has invaded the world with her errors. And if we have not yet seen the complete fulfillment of the final part of this prophecy, we are going toward it little by little with great strides. If we do not reject the path of sin, hatred, revenge, injustice, violations of the rights of the human person, immorality and violence, etc. And let us not say that it is God who is punishing us in this way; on the contrary it is people themselves who are preparing their own punishment. In his kindness God warns us and calls us to the right path, while respecting the freedom he has given us; hence people are responsible.[3]

But did you examine the entire text of the Third Secret word for word, or did you just ask about its general meaning?

We read the text carefully and slowly, in the presence of the bishop of Leiria-Fatima, who served as a witness. After all, Sister Lucia herself was rereading for the first time a text she had written fifty-six years earlier. While she read it over, I didn't make any remarks. The question I asked her was whether she had made the connection between the "Bishop dressed in White" and the attempted assassination of John Paul II. Did the Third Secret concern the popes in general, or did it relate in some special way to John Paul II?

And how did she answer?

She said that as soon as she had learned of the assassination attempt, she had connected it with the Third Secret. True, Paul VI was also targeted by a fanatic, who managed to wound him slightly. But there was no actual bullet, no literal agreement with the Third Secret.

Excuse me, Your Eminence, but in the vision, the pope is pierced through by various projectiles, and then dies. But John Paul II survived.

You're right. The pope didn't die. But that's actually the crucial point. It's a historical or medico-historical point, but it also affects the theological interpretation of the prophecy. From a medical and historical point of view, the pope did fall and was on the very threshold of death. When he got to Gemelli, he was already lifeless. He had lost a lot of blood and his condition was desperate. Once, when I was lunching with the pope, his secretary, Stanislaw Dziwisz, who is currently the cardinal archbishop of Kraków, related the sequence of natural and (I would even say) providential, if not supernatural, events that took place in those terrible hours. At a certain point, they even decided to prepare a death certificate.

I knew that Cardinal Dziwisz gave the pope the last rites, but I didn't know about the death certificate.

They *intended* to prepare a death certificate. My point is not that they actually issued the physical document, but just that they had come to a point where there no longer seemed to be any hope of saving the pope's life. As fate would have it, Dr. Castiglioni, the chief surgeon, was away at the time. But Providence had plans of its own. You see, Professor Crucitti, who happened to be walking around Rome at that very moment, was visited by an inspiration: "I'll go see how my patients in Gemelli are doing." His children have told me that he had no visit to Gemelli scheduled for that day. Crucitti just showed up at Gemelli unannounced and was practically dragged to the operating room: "Go up to the operating room. They've shot the pope." Miraculously, they were able to resuscitate him and proceed with the operation, which lasted for hours (it did not finish until 10:00 p.m.). As we all know, the outcome was positive. The pope's life was saved in extremis. It was as if he had died and then been snatched back from the very jaws of death.

Your Eminence, what you say tallies with the account left us by the surgeons who operated on John Paul II. The pope had suffered cardiac arrest. Professor Giancarlo Castiglioni, who was head of the Institute for Clinical Surgery, was at a convention in Milan and returned to Rome only after the surgery had already begun. The operation was performed by Castiglioni's students under the guidance of Francesco Crucitti, who at the time was director of the Institute for Surgical Semiotics, a research center specializing in surgical methodology. The situation was obviously highly stressful. The clinical file, which was drawn up after the operation, reads like the description of a battlefield. Operation number 750, file number 364465, was signed sometime during the night by Professors Castiglioni, Crucitti, Salgarello, Wiel Marin, and Zucchetti, as well as by Dr. Ronconi. This is what we learn from the medical report, which shows signs that its authors were in a state of very understandable agitation (for example, in the first draft, the name Wojtyla is illegible): The bullet had perforated various sections of the pope's intestine, but it had very narrowly missed vital organs such as the liver and the spleen. It had not struck the spinal column, but only the sacrum. There was a vertical incision running down the pope's whole stomach, from the sternum to the pelvis. In addition, the patient had lost a lot of blood, was in a state of shock, had abnormally low blood pressure, and was suffering from tachycardia. The pope was kept alive during those desperate hours by a continual supply of liquids, together with constant blood transfusions, which were necessary to replenish the blood he had lost through the gunshot wounds. No less than sixty-six centimeters of the intestine were perforated. All of this makes it clear that John Paul II's life was indeed saved by a miracle. And now let's move to the theological aspect of the prophecy.

As Cardinal Ratzinger correctly explained, a prophecy, even a catastrophic or apocalyptic one, cannot be inevitable. Our Lady called for "Penance, Penance, Penance!" Prayer and penance are stronger than evil and bullets. Prophecy does not predict some inevitable fate that is deterministically bound to happen no matter what. Otherwise, we would be at the mercy of dark forces dangling us over an abyss of nothingness.

That would make absolutely no sense given everything that we know about theology, spirituality, or the Church. Prophecy gives us a glimpse of the baleful consequences of certain individual or collective actions or behaviors. It gives us a glimpse of them—but this doesn't mean that they are necessarily bound to occur. On the contrary, prophecy is an urgent invitation to conversion, penance, and prayer, and the point is that these things have the power to change the course of history. The mistake made by some of the Fatimists after the publication of the Third Secret was to give the text a literal, fatalistic interpretation. They hastily concluded that the Vatican had withheld the Third Secret until the year 2000 because John Paul II had survived the assassination attempt, whereas, in their view, the pope's actual death was a requirement for the prophecy to be fulfilled. They seemed to assume that everything is governed by chance, and not by the God who "delivers us from evil." The freedom to do evil is not the last word. True freedom is the freedom to be on God's side.

So you explained all that to Sister Lucia and she agreed with your interpretation?

Of course, even though I didn't put it in exactly these terms. Lucia vigorously emphasized the power of prayer and underscored her rock-solid conviction that it was impossible for the hearts of Jesus and Mary to turn a deaf ear to our supplications.

THE ENIGMA OF JOHN PAUL I

Of course you wouldn't have put it in just those terms. The word "White" is capitalized: "The Bishop dressed in White." Now, could "White" be a reference to Albino Luciani? On July 11, 1977, Luciani, then still Patriarch of Venice, visited Coimbra. Father Diego Lorenzi, who at the time was Luciani's personal secretary, told me that he, Luciani, and Sister Lucia spoke for about two hours. "When the Patriarch left the room, his face was pale. He was white as a sheet." Luciani himself spoke of Lucia somewhat jocosely: "She's tiny, sprightly, and pretty talkative." Cut to Lent of the following year (1978). According to the testimony published by my fellow Vatican watcher Andrea Tornielli, Albino Luciani's brother, Edoardo, revealed that, while on vacation in Canale d'Agordo, Albino was very preoccupied, avoided company, and seemed anxious and ill at ease. His family asked him what was bothering him, and he replied: "I can't stop thinking about what Sister Lucia told me." He didn't elaborate. Twice he started to say "Sister Lucia told me . . ." but then broke off in midsentence. What can the visionary have said to the future Pope John Paul I? And wasn't his ascent to the papacy a crucifixion, humanly speaking? Luciani was the first pope to appear without the tiara—as a simple "Bishop dressed in White." How short-lived his pontificate was! It was like a photograph taken of someone passing in front of a mirror, to quote from a passage in the Third Secret.

Sister Lucia never mentioned Pope John Paul I. When I met with her the first time, she immediately and unequivocally connected the Third Secret with John Paul II. It was only during the third meeting, which took place on December 9, 2003, that I broached the question of Pope John Paul I.

I think we had better adhere to a clear time line. Let's stick with the second meeting, which took place on November 17, 2001. This meeting resulted in an unusual document that received almost no attention. I'm referring to the long press release that was published in both L'Osservatore Romano *and* Avvenire.

That's correct. A summary of the meeting was drafted, and it was then signed both by me and by Maria Lucia De Jesus e Do Coração Imaculado. There were two questions—or, if you will, suspicions. Had the Holy See really published the complete text of the third part of the Secret? While the world was still reeling from 9/11, newspapers both in Italy and abroad were publishing stories about revelations from Sister Lucia, reporting claims that she had written warnings to the pope, and spreading apocalyptic interpretations of the Fatima message. On top of that, some people were repeating the charge that the pope hadn't yet consecrated Russia to the Immaculate Heart of Mary, as Our Lady had asked him to do through the three shepherd children.

I found Sister Lucia in excellent spirits. She was very lively and responsive. "Everything"—and when she said this, she paused to give the word its full weight—"has been published; there are no more secrets." This was her message to people who talk and write about "new revelations": "None of it is true. If I had had new revelations, I wouldn't have divulged them to anyone. I would have relayed them directly to the Holy Father." She was pained by the rampant speculation about the Secret. Her sadness over this idle curiosity is reflected in the memorial of Lucia recently written by her prioress, Sister Maria Celina. Before the Third Secret was revealed, Lucia used to say sadly: "If they would just devote their energy to living out the real essence of the message, which has already been revealed. . . . All they care about is what hasn't yet been said, rather than the fulfillment of Our Lady's request for prayer and penance." After the Secret had been revealed, some people began to doubt the genuineness of the text. Lucia's Carmelite superior in Coimbra told her about this doubt: "They're saying that there's another secret." With a sigh, Lucia replied: "Well, if they know what it is, then let them tell us. For my part, I don't know about any other secrets. Some people are never satisfied. Let's not pay them any mind." During the second meeting (which lasted for two hours), Lucia revealed to me a hitherto unknown detail. "During the vision, Our Lady was radiating light, and she held a heart in her right hand and a rosary in her left."

What does the heart in Our Lady's right hand signify?

According to Lucia, "it is a sign of saving love. Her Heart is a sure refuge. Devotion to the Immaculate Heart of Mary is the means of salvation God has bestowed to help the Church and the world through these difficult times." Lucia was also in full agreement with the theological commentary Cardinal Ratzinger wrote to accompany the publication of the last part of the Secret.

Meanwhile, though, people were gathering signatures in an effort to compel the pope to consecrate Russia to the Immaculate Heart.

I told Sister Lucia about this. "Given the petition's stated purpose," she replied, "the Carmelite community simply threw it away. I've already said that the consecration Our Lady wished for was performed in 1984, and that it was accepted by Heaven."

We'll come back to this point later. Is it true that Sister Lucia was worried about the direction the Church seemed to be taking?

According to some very imaginative writers, Lucia wasn't sleeping, but was spending all her nights and days in prayer. Sister Lucia herself was stunned: "It's not true. How could I pray during the day if I didn't rest at night? I can't believe all the things they imagine that I say and do. Let them read my writings: there they'll find what Our Lady counseled and requested them to do. What will save the world is prayer, penance, and great faith in God."

Sister Lucia was good at negotiating the pitfalls of communication. She didn't need to be some kind of oracle predicting the latest news before it happened. Now, what do you think Albino Luciani and Sister Lucia talked about on July 11, 1977?

We didn't discuss Pope John Paul I until our December 9, 2003, meeting. Sister Lucia told me that she and Luciani had talked for a long time—almost five hours, according to her version of events—about the situation of the contemporary Church and the importance of courageous Christian witness. They both felt that such witness was needed if the Church was going to respond to the challenges of indifference and ignorance. I should add that we read to Lucia the account—the minutes, you might say—in which the patriarch himself had summed up the substance of his meeting with her. Smiling, she confirmed that the text was an exact record of what she and Luciani had discussed during their meeting. She said she was prepared to sign the text, provided we would translate it into Portuguese. So we decided to undertake a translation with Father Luis Kondor, the vice postulator of the cause for the beatification of Jacinta and Francisco.

So now we have another completely, or almost completely, unknown text. You speak of an "account" and "minutes." Was this text an article of Luciani's? Was it a sketch for a chapter in his memoirs or a passage from his personal diary?

What we brought to Lucia was a typewritten text bearing the patriarch's signature. In all likelihood, it was published in January 1978. I think it appeared in a magazine entitled *Il Cuore della Madre,* but I could be wrong about that. The text is outstanding from the literary point of view and is typical of Albino Luciani's style as a catechist and a pastor. It is fresh and immediate. In fact, I almost want to describe it as "sunny."

It's amazing to me that people are surprised that he became pope. Sister Lucia read the text in Portuguese and then put her signature to it. She signed it on December 27, 2003—so just a few days after my third meeting with her. Here is Luciani's account of the one-on-one meeting between himself and Sister Lucia:

> On Monday, July 11, I and a few priests from Venice and environs concelebrated Mass in the Carmelite church in Coimbra, a Portuguese city of about 100,000 people. Since cardinals have permission to enter the cloister, I went immediately after Mass to meet with the entire community of nuns (twenty-three professed sisters and novices). I then had a long talk with Sister Lucia dos Santos. Sister Lucia is seventy, but she wears her age well, as she herself told me with a smile. She didn't repeat Pius IX's quip: "I carry them quite well; none of them has fallen on me yet." Nevertheless, her joviality, her fluent manner of speaking, the passionate interest she shows in everything that concerns the contemporary Church and its problems are signs that show her spiritual youthfulness. I am more or less proficient in Portuguese, since, apart from a very sketchy study of the language, I once spent a couple of weeks in Brazil. Even if I were completely ignorant of the language, though, I would still have understood Sister Lucia. She stressed how important it was for today's Christians, especially seminarians and novices, to be serious in their commitment to belonging unreservedly to God. She spoke to me with great energy and conviction of *freiras, padres e cristiãos a firme cabeça* (sisters, priests, and Christians who have their heads on straight). She is as radical as the saints: with her it is *ou toudo ou nada*, all or nothing, if you are serious about belonging to God. Sister Lucia did not talk to me about the apparitions. I limited myself to asking her about

the famous "dance of the sun." She did not see it. On October 13, 1917, 70,000 people watched for ten minutes straight as the sun changed colors, spun about on its axis, and then plummeted toward the earth. But Lucia, along with her two companions, saw something different: They didn't see the sun move, but they did see the Holy Family standing next to it. Then they beheld a succession of images of Mary in the guise of Our Lady of Sorrows and Our Lady of Mount Carmel.

At this point, someone might ask: How come a cardinal is so interested in private revelations? Doesn't he know that everything is already contained in the Gospel? Doesn't he realize that even Church-approved private revelations are not articles of faith? I am perfectly aware of these truths. But it is precisely one of the articles of faith we find in the Gospel that certain extraordinary signs will accompany believers in Christ (Mk 16:17).

It's become quite the fashion today to "search the signs of the times." In fact, we're suffering from inflation and an epidemic of "signs." So I have no qualms about looking to the sign that was given on October 13, 1917, which even anticlericals and nonbelievers confirmed had really happened. And it's good to look beyond the sign and think about the things that the sign is meant to convey. What are these things?

First: That we should repent of our sins and stop offending the Lord.

Second: That we should pray. Prayer is the medium of communication with God. Today, however, the human communications media (TV, radio, movies, newspapers) shamelessly impose their will, and they seem bent on getting rid of prayer altogether. The proverb *ceci tuera cela* (one thing drives out another) appears to be coming true nowadays. Moreover, it wasn't me, but Karl Rahner, who wrote: "Even within the

Church, man is devoting himself exclusively to temporal things. This is no longer a matter of a legitimate option, but of apostasy and a total collapse of faith."

Third: We should pray the holy Rosary. Naaman, the great Syrian general, disdained the simple bath in the Jordan suggested to him by Elisha. Some people act like Naaman: "I am a great theologian, a mature Christian, who breathes the Bible with both lungs and sweats liturgy from every pore—and they tell me to pray the *Rosary?*" And yet the fifteen mysteries of the Rosary are biblical; the Pater, the Ave Maria, and the Gloria are Bible passages transformed into prayer, and they are good for the soul. Bible study solely for the sake of scholarship could puff up the soul and leave it in a state of sterile aridity. Bible scholars who have lost their faith are hardly a rare breed.

Fourth: Hell exists and it's possible to end up there. At Fatima, Our Lady taught this prayer: "O my Jesus, forgive us our sins, save us from the fires of hell, lead all souls to heaven, especially those in most need of thy mercy." There are a lot of important things in this world, but none is so important as meriting Paradise by means of a good life. It's not Fatima that says this, but the Gospel: "For what will it profit a man, if he gains the whole world and forfeits his life? Or what shall a man give in return for his life?" (Mt 16:26).

We imagine Lucia saying to Luciani: "You will become pope. Your pontificate will be short and painful." I don't know why we're all convinced that Lucia foretold Luciani's election to the papacy.

That's right. It's a mystery created by the media. Or maybe it's a lopsided interpretation of the testimony you cited earlier. Who knows. Once, during a program on the Rai network, Corrado Augias said that "it's better not to investigate the mysteries of the faith." The fact is that reporters sometimes get lost in mysteries or pseudomysteries. They tear the old ones down in order to build up new ones in their place. I asked Sister Lucia a very specific question about the prediction of Luciani's election, and her reply was that she couldn't recall having foretold anything of the sort. She only said that when she was talking with the other sisters about Cardinal Luciani's visit, she spontaneously exclaimed: "If he were elected pope, I think he would make a good one." I see nothing surprising in her exclamation. I confess that I was attracted by John Paul I. He had a talent for reaching out through the camera to touch people's hearts. In fact, the bishop of Belluno-Feltre, the Salesian Vincenzo Savio, together with emeritus Bishop Maffeo Ducoli, has recently opened the cause of beatification for Pope Luciani (Pope John Paul I). I won't deny that there is a lot of literature and a lot of speculation, or, if you prefer, a convergence of evidence, that points to the idea that Lucia predicted that the then patriarch of Venice would become pope. But in 2003 Lucia merely pointed out to me the bench in the parlor where Cardinal Luciani had sat and recounted to me their very full conversation concerning the problems of the Church.

Sister Lucia was ninety-five.

Yes, she was ninety-five, and she had a verve, a good humor, that kept the entire community of nuns cheerful. She was a likeable old chatterbox. Sister Maria Celina of Jesus Crucified, her superior, told me some amusing anecdotes. In 2004, for example, she was dissatisfied with the spiritual exercises preached by a Brazilian bishop. She thought his talks were too long and she wasn't able to follow them because she was so hard of hearing. She gave Sister Maria Celina three gentle taps on the forehead with her fist and asked: "What ever possessed you to invite a Brazilian to give the retreat?" Finally, the prioress told Lucia that her "preacherly torments" were over. Lucia exclaimed, "Thanks be to God." Then, during recreation, she invited the other sisters to celebrate with her and to clap their hands for joy. Even during our conversations she wouldn't miss an opportunity for a joke, for example, about the fact that I am a Salesian or that I am devoted to Mary, Help of Christians. Once, when I told her that I had spoken about Our Lady of Fatima in Lourdes, she remarked that it's a bad idea to confuse Our Ladies. Our Lady of Lourdes, she said, would surely take it amiss that I had spoken of Our Lady of Fatima on her turf.

What's your theory about the prediction?

I think Lucia was struck by the meekness of Albino Luciani, by his disarming smile, and his solid grounding in doctrine. She made a joke, but that is something very different from an actual prophecy.

ONE ENVELOPE, ONE SECRET

We've already discussed the large envelope bearing the seal of the Congregation for the Doctrine of the Faith. This envelope contained another envelope, marked "1960," with four pages in Sister Lucia's own hand. Italian author Marco Tosatti has constructed a whole book around the hypothesis of "The Unrevealed Secret" (Il segreto non svelato). The theory that there were two texts of the Third Secret has been revived countless times. Precisely because of this reinterpretation of events, Sister Lucia placed the following sentence at the end of the Second Secret in her memoirs: "In Portugal, the dogma of the faith will always be preserved, etc."[1] The "etc." is the Third Secret. Father René Laurentin, an internationally famed Mariologist and the dean of Lourdes scholars, believed that this reference to Portugal's faith was followed by a prediction of the apostasy of other large, traditionally Catholic countries. One day in Rome he pointed out to me the discrepancy between the dates when the message is supposed to have been transferred to Rome: April 4, 1957, or April 16, 1957? Alfredo Cardinal Ottaviani stated that the Secret was written on a single sheet of paper. So we would be talking about twenty to twenty-five lines in toto, whereas the text presented in the press room of the Holy See on June 26, 2000, consisted of sixty-two lines. In other words, it added up to four pages, not one. These are small, feeble bits of evidence, which neither prove nor disprove anything. On June 7, 1981, John Paul II personally composed an Act of Entrustment to the Immaculate Heart of Mary. In July, while still recovering at Gemelli, he read the file they had brought him from the Vatican. Couldn't it be that the first document contained Our Lady's words, while the second contained the description of the vision?

There is no "first document." There was never any such text in the archives of the Holy Office. In order to access documents there, you needed three keys. In those days, the office of prefect of the Congregation had not yet been invented. The pope himself was head of the Holy Office. So I'm not sure what Cardinal Ottaviani was talking about. I do know two things, though. First, as far as the custodians of the archives can remember, there were never two separate envelopes. There was always just one. Second, we have the word, better, the official confirmation, of Sister Lucia: "Is this the Third Secret, and is this the only text of it?" "Yes, this is the Third Secret, and I never wrote any other." Hard-core Fatimists, like the followers of Father Nicholas Gruner and the readers of his magazine, *Fatima Crusader,* are in for a disappointment.

Indeed. The unknown text supposedly foretells a catastrophe: an unprecedented chastisement with devastating consequences for the Church, the faithful, and the hierarchy. It's a scenario that pits cardinals against cardinals and that depicts a decline of faith that opens up the floodgates of hell on earth.

It's all very sensational, not to mention a bit gloomy, but it is completely unsupported by any documentary evidence.

And yet, despite the absence of documentary proof, there is an endless flood of books with titles like The Unrevealed Secret *and* The Fourth Secret of Fatima. *You have explained that it was the pope himself who personally made the decision to go public with the Secret, and that it was the CDF that managed the whole operation. So there aren't two envelopes or two secrets. In Sister Lucia's mind, moreover, the date 1960 had only a temporal, not a meta-temporal or prophetic, much less apocalyptic, meaning. So from your point of view, Your Eminence, it's possible to tie up all the loose ends and to clarify the whole matter. And yet, according to people such as Antonio*

Socci, author of a pamphlet entitled Il quarto segreto di Fatima *(The Fourth Secret of Fatima), what seems like a straight line turns out to be crooked, apparently straightforward facts are really convoluted distortions, and every semblance of clarity sinks into a disturbing murkiness.*

The people you mention are merely dusting off the well-worn claim that the Third Secret isn't about the attempt to assassinate the pope on May 13, 1981. Instead, the Third Secret is supposedly the continuation of the words "In Portugal, the dogma of the faith will always be preserved, etc." The Fatimists assert that the missing words are explosive. They say that there is, or allegedly is, another text after the "etc." They also have no qualms about contending that the commentary shouldn't have been based on Sister Lucia's third memoir, but on the fourth memoir, which was her last writing. In the Fourth Memoir, Sister Lucia cites the Virgin as saying: "Don't tell this to anyone, except Francisco; you can tell him."

You're stealing my thunder, Your Eminence. According to Socci and others, the "etc.," as well as the mention of Francisco, is an allusion to the text that the Vatican has supposedly refused to reveal. The alleged reason for this refusal is that publication would backfire against the Church, since the text putatively predicts a worldwide apostasy of the Church—an "Apocalypse Now" *for Rome. Rome, the prediction supposedly says, will lose the faith and become the throne of the Antichrist. I think I smell the "smoke of Satan" Paul VI spoke of. Needless to say, Your Eminence, they also try to put you in the hot seat. They accuse you of "embarrassed evasiveness," reserve, and "fidelity to a mafia-like code of silence."*

That's absolutely crazy. Look, are you claiming that the prophecy of Fatima is about the apostasy of the Church of *Rome?* That Fatima is a prediction of Rome's transformation into the throne of the Antichrist? Despite the love Our Lady has for the pope, and the popes for Our Lady? I'm talking about *all* the twentieth-century popes, including Joseph Ratzinger, Benedict XVI. Anyone can write books based on conspiracy theories, on biased interpretations. Anybody can take sentences out of context and present them as clues to some supposed plot to avoid divulging the truth and to transmit it in a code that only the initiates can understand. No, the whole theory you allude to is a fabrication. And this supposedly factual account—I mean the one you've mentioned, though there are many others that employ the same tactics—is actually the sort of device the Masons used to invent to discredit the Church. I'm amazed that journalists and writers who claim to be Catholic let themselves be taken in.

So the theory says that there are two texts of the Third Secret. One was revealed in the year 2000; the other remained in the papal apartments, where Pius XII had brought it and John XXIII and Paul VI had each read it in his turn. This second text is referred to as the so-called Capovilla File, named after Pope John XXIII's secretary, Monsignor Loris Capovilla.

These people look at everything through the magnifying glass of their biases. As a result they latch on to the most unbelievable things. They seize on the fact that, in the published version of the Secret, the Virgin does not speak directly to the shepherd children. The Secret contains only a description, a vision recounted in the third person. This is supposed to prove that someone took it upon himself to excise the Virgin's words because they were considered too dangerous. And what makes them so absolutely certain that this "file" remained in the papal "apartments" (I suppose in a drawer of the pope's nightstand)?

You tell me.

The part of the text where the Virgin speaks in the first person wasn't censored, for the simple reason that it never existed. The text these people talk about just doesn't exist. I am not toeing some party line here. I'm basing my statement on Sister Lucia's own direct confirmation that the Third Secret is none other than the text that was published in the year 2000. What are we supposed to be censoring here? We know perfectly well that tampering is forbidden; that we aren't allowed to line up the events to fit our preconceived notions. The media have doggedly refused to resign themselves to the fact that the prophecy is no longer open to the future, but refers to something that now belongs to the past. They are unwilling to accept the obvious. The part that remains valid, and that is still just as urgently relevant as ever, is Our Lady's message, which is what is most important about the prophecy in the first place.

Now that Sister Lucia has died, she can no longer leave her complete and exhaustive testimony to posterity. According to Socci, "the few words she is quoted as saying in the officially published documents are objectively lacking in credibility. Thus, Sister Lucia's most eloquent statements are the ones she never got to make."

And so, on top of everything else, we are liars, liars who knowingly perpetrate falsehood. What do they expect? That a holy old Carmelite nun would appear on TV to be briefed by journalists? That she would appear live on CNN, or some other network, and face a firing line of questions on an issue, or an encounter, that had turned her life upside down? "The few words": That's rich. From the time she learned to read and write, Lucia spent almost seventy years writing! Not only did she author several books numbering hundreds of pages apiece, but she answered thousands of letters as well. If the truth had been otherwise, don't you think someone would have exploited the discrepancy to embarrass the Church? No, the true account of what happened is the one we've been trying patiently and methodically to piece together here. We need to maintain a strict respect for what Sister Lucia told us, told me, without forcing anything. Anyone who doesn't do that shows nothing but contempt for the visionary herself.

When you returned to Rome after the first mission, you related to the pope the substance of your conversation with Sister Lucia. How did he react?

First of all, it confirmed his judgment that the time was right to publish the Third Secret in order to calm the storm of speculation. He also took Lucia's response as a confirmation of the mission, the mission of suffering, which determined the shape of his life.

In her own unpretentious way, Lucia put her seal on the pope's Via Crucis, even though she kept insisting: "It's not my job to interpret; the interpretation is up to the Church and the pope. I'm just telling the facts, what I saw and what I felt and perceived." I'd like to point out that Lucia never felt like a prophetess. She never felt inspired. And even when she assures us that she is transmitting the *ipsissima verba,* the very words, of Our Lady, her personal sincerity is on the line. Lucia is sure of just one thing: the content of her message. There is an *oeconomia silentii,* that is, a wise policy of silence, a special care, surrounding the publication of the Fatima documents. "Usually," Lucia writes, "God also gives the recipient of his revelations an intimate, loving perception of their meaning. But I don't dare speak of that, because I am afraid of being deceived in my imagination. It seems to me very easy to fall into such deception." And in the Fourth Memoir, which is the most ample of the four, she explains that she is going to tell everything, "except the part of the 'Secret' that for now I am not permitted to reveal." She also writes: "Not a few people have expressed astonishment over the gift of memory that God has deigned to bestow on me. By an act of his infinite kindness, I do have an uncommonly good memory. But, since we are dealing with supernatural things, this should not come as a surprise, because such realities leave an imprint on the soul that is almost impossible to forget. At any rate, their meaning is never forgotten, unless God himself wills that it should be." In these passages, Sister Lucia shows that she is no tyro when it comes to analyzing the workings of memory and the complexities involved in the vision of otherworldly realities. She is rereading her faith in the light of a unique and singular experience. Even Cardinal Ratzinger's interpretation of the Secret, while obviously enjoying a high degree of authority, is not a dogma of faith. Rather, it simply offers the world's Catholics a theological framework in which to make sense of the mystery.

Back to John Paul II. The Holy Father said just a few words at the time, but they struck me forcibly, because it was clear that Sister Lucia had reinforced his conviction of having been called to a mission of suffering. Wasn't his greatest encyclical on the mystery of suffering? Although he didn't die in the assassination attempt, in some sense he did experience death, because day after day he offered his life for the good of the Church. In a way, he did undergo a daily death on account of the shooting. In all likelihood, even the Parkinson's was a result of the assassination attempt. It also left Wojtyla feeling even more closely connected with Our Lady of Fatima. He had the bullet set inside Our Lady's crown in the Cova da Iria. The pope also laid at her feet the ring he had received as a gift from Cardinal Stephan Wyszynski, the primate of Poland.

The most amazing thing about your account is who its central protagonists are: three uneducated shepherd children; three good, mischievously playful children, whose life consisted of their flock, their innocent games, and their penances.

John Paul II, who beatified Jacinta and Francisco, spoke of them as "two small flames" that had been kindled to light up the world. Jesus made children the central theme of preaching as he wandered about Palestine. The child is the "teacher of the man," because he shows the grown-up a kind of maturity that consists in docility to God's wisdom, which, as we know, transcends and challenges the ways of men. You journalists have told the life of John Paul II as a great evangelizer. He wrote the "Gospel of work," of the "family," of "peace," of the "defense of human life," of the "woman," and the "child." For anyone who has ears to hear, his life is an unforgettably eloquent embodiment of the teaching of the little ones. Great Mariologists, drawing on the insights of psychology, have thoroughly researched the role of children in Marian apparitions. Their conclusion is that children are infinitely more likely to be true and reliable witnesses than are adults.

Are you saying it is better to be ignorant than learned?

Uneducated children are much more likely to have uncluttered minds. They are like a blank slate in the hands of God. In any case, the shepherd children of Fatima had fresh minds that were able to receive Our Lady's message and transmit it unaltered. This is why their accounts seem so simple and direct, why they have that uncomplicated, straightforward quality you find only in children or in people who are as ingenuous as children.

The obvious question, then, is this: When do you know if an apparition comes from God?

The answer has to do with the nature of so-called private revelations. I'm not an expert on the subject, but you have to make an initial distinction between "visions," which are not necessarily external to the visionary, and "apparitions," in which God causes some external reality to be perceived by the senses. In the history of the Church, visions seem to be the preserve of the saints, whereas apparitions (I mean the approved ones) seem to happen to individuals whom we could regard as novices in the spiritual life.

Okay, but isn't there the risk of mistaking illusions, or even hallucinations, for apparitions?

Hallucinations are due to a mental disturbance, which is induced either by some imbalance in the body or by some chemical substance introduced into the body from the outside. In the most extreme cases, the victim is trapped in a perverse, diabolical circle he can no longer break out of. True visions or apparitions come to people who are totally balanced. True visionaries don't contradict themselves and, when they become adults, they are even aware of the fragility of their experience. They may recount what happened to them in different ways, but the essential point is always the same. This was the case with Sister Lucia. Let's not forget the written accounts of the apparitions either. When you read them correctly, you see that they don't contradict the teaching of the Church. Rather, they're a sort of "Gospel in action," and that is a point in favor of their genuineness. For its part, the Church has always proceeded with great caution, taking all the time it needed to evaluate the evidence. Just think: According to contemporary accounts, the first bishop to set foot in the Cova da Iria was the bishop of Fatima, and he didn't go there until October 1926. He went in person to verify whether the large numbers of the faithful (or the curious) who were by now pouring into Fatima made it necessary to provide for a proper supply of water. He requested that a well be dug, and he gave instructions for the spiritual assistance of the pilgrims. This is just an example of how the Church, in the person of the local bishop, has always been reluctant to accept a vision or an apparition without minute examination. There is a passage from the *Catechism of the Catholic Church* that makes another important point: "Guided by the Magisterium of the Church, the sense of the faithful is able to discern and accept what in these revelations is an authentic message of Christ and his saints for the Church."

MYSTERIES BEYOND OUR KEN

Psychologists warn us not to take everything that comes out of the mouth of visionaries as if it were the Gospel truth. After all, visionaries are only human, which means that they are subject to change. Moreover, this process of change can lead to mental disturbance, or perhaps to embarrassing recantations. The great theologian Karl Rahner writes that, in assessing claims of private revelations, we can't "rule out the possibility of illusions, false interpretations, or deformations, even in cases where the substance is undeniably authentic." Some speak of "a self-image projected by the unconscious mind." Others highlight the fact that so-called visionaries sometimes face the terrifying prospect of "the irretrievable loss of their own identity." Could this be the reason that for centuries the Church has defended itself against visionaries, why it has regarded them as dangerous fanatics, and why it has sought to cast its faith in Christ in the most rational and objective form possible? If I may put it a bit epigrammatically: Haven't the visionaries of yesterday been replaced by the theologians of today?

Well, let's not overstate the case. If apparitions weren't a sign of a different reality, a call to turn our eyes toward a higher plane, they wouldn't generate pilgrimages, conversions, or acts of prayer. I'm not at all opposed to the kind of fervent religiosity that seeks to open doors to the supernatural. We need to avoid presumptuous, prejudiced condemnations of the feeling for the miraculous. The pathologies investigated by the psychologists are not the whole story. In fact, there are humanistic psychologists who have offered some pretty subtle analyses of phenomena such as visions and apparitions. For my part, when I met Sister Lucia, I found her to be a totally balanced person without any hang-ups. Although the psychological approach is important, it's not the only one that's relevant here. You also have to look at things from the angle of sociology and anthropology. Now, both of these disciplines agree that, however indispensable the psychological approach may be for understanding a visionary's personality and the mechanisms of his unconscious, it isn't sufficient to account for apparitions. The point I'm driving at here is that the mind has a free zone that is open to the irruption of the sacred. In a postmodern context, faith probably needs a maternal, affective dimension. This is why Our Lady is the central figure in the apparitions. This has a whole range of important pastoral implications. Thanks to Mary, God is not some remote, inaccessible, silent spectator of individual and collective history.

At the end of the beatification Mass for Jacinta and Francisco, Cardinal Angelo Sodano divulged the substance of the Third Secret. His address was heard by a million people in Fatima and was broadcast around the world on TV. Had the CDF prepared Cardinal Sodano's remarks beforehand?

Of course. The prefect of the Congregation and his staff worked out the basic interpretive approach to the message. They also made it clear that at some point they would produce a special document to comment on the Fatima event in its historical and theological context.

For the first time ever, the custodian of the Catholic faith, Cardinal Joseph Ratzinger, was making public statements about a private revelation. This alone would be enough to underscore the exceptional nature of the event. After all, some years earlier, the same Ratzinger had said: "Fatima will not be the origin of the apocalypse. That is impossible. No apparition is indispensable to the faith, because Revelation ended with Jesus Christ. Secret

messages add nothing to what a Christian needs to know of Revelation."
Your Eminence, I have the distinct impression that if Ratzinger had had his
druthers, the Secret would have stayed a secret. Or am I mistaken?

I think you are. Pope Benedict XIV had already given the Church a
carefully worked out distinction between public and private revelation.
So it wasn't as if we were jumping over a cliff with no safety net. Moreover, Cardinal Ratzinger was not opposed to revealing the Third Secret.
He didn't have any doubts or objections. The assassination attempt and
the pope's illness were signs. The last postscript to the shooting was the
pope's offering forgiveness to Ali Agca at the Rebibbia prison on December 27, 1983. We were almost overwhelmed by an abundance of very
meaningful signs. So why not transmit the call of Fatima to the broader
Christian community? After all, it is the call to conversion, prayer, and
penance issued by Our Lord's Mother herself. The Fatima message is saturated with the Gospel.

What if it had been up to Tarcisio Bertone?

By temperament, I'm much more of a take-charge kind of person. So
I would have published the secret without any hesitation. In any case,
the publication didn't halt the flood of interpretations, and a lot of
words were spent on the subject in every conceivable forum, often pretty
fruitlessly. The revelation of the Secret was a great gift for Catholics
everywhere, a great gift for everyone who is devoted to Our Lady. It was
even a gift for nonbelievers.

Just now, you mentioned Prospero Lambertini, Pope Benedict XIV. Writing
at the end of the eighteenth century, he worked out the classic account of the
difference between private revelations and public Revelation:

> *In authorizing a private revelation, the Church merely consents to its*
> *divulgation for the edification and good of the faithful. Even when*
> *such revelations are approved by the Church, however, they cannot be*

given an assent of Catholic faith. Rather, such revelations fall under the competence of human prudence. Thus, they can at most be assented to with human faith, insofar as they are probable or piously credible. One can thus refuse one's assent to, and ignore, these revelations, so long as one does so with the appropriate reserve, for good reasons, and without feelings of contempt.

There you have it: Private revelations are at most "piously credible" and humanly reliable.

Fatima is different, though. With Fatima, all the elements seem linked together in a compelling (and violent) whole of overwhelming proportions. The pope was always convinced that Mary had saved his life. Then, with all the world watching, he countenanced the application of the kernel of the Third Secret to himself. So the decision to go public with the Secret looks to me like a pretty bold shift; "gamble" is another word that comes to mind. Or maybe you could put it in terms of a dynamic impulse of the heart, an inspired guess, a leap of intuition. In any case, it was something that reflected the heart, the charism, and the mysticism of Karol Wojtyla.

A leap of intuition? I would call it the end point of a process of reflection, a process of internalizing the mystery, which started during his hospitalization at Gemelli. Don't forget that the "pre-shooting" John Paul II had always had a deep mystical sense. As he wrote in one of his later poems, "Suffering entered into me like a plow penetrating the ground." Karol Wojtyla's whole biography is defined by three coordinates: gift, mystery, and suffering. His entire life echoed the martyrdom of the twentieth-century Church and the suffering of the giants of the persecuted and martyred "Church of silence," such as Cardinals Wyszynski, Beran, Midszenty, and Stepinac. Think of it: The Church, even entire nations, were massacred in Hitler's concentration camps. Jews, Poles, millions of people from other nations were slaughtered by the Nazis and then by the Communists. Next came the period of official atheism, the Soviet gulags, the cries emerging from the silence of the catacombs. This whole series of events radically transformed John Paul II. Moreover, the shooting involved him as firsthand protagonist in this same history as the Vicar of Christ on earth, the shepherd of the universal Church. The whole suffering, martyred Church took flesh in him and became intertwined with his own personal pain.

It is as if the shooting had been written in his destiny, inscribed in the trajectory of his existence. So we have to ask ourselves (with a certain apprehension): Who armed Ali Agca? It's as if we were dealing here with an inscrutable "providential" plan. Fatima is a mixture of the heavenly and the earthly. For example, immediately after the shooting, a nun who happened to be called Lucia blocked and tackled Ali Agca. Amidst his ravings, John Paul II's would-be assassin would say that he felt like the plaything of some obscure mystery.

Look, that sort of language simplifies and distorts reality. It isolates certain aspects of a whole complex experience in an attempt to evade responsibility. Who armed evil? Evil exists. Pope Benedict XVI has reminded us of its existence in one of his richest and most powerful addresses. During his visit to Auschwitz-Birkenau on May 28, 2006, he talked about what happens when the god of violence kills faith:

> Where was God in those days? Why was he silent? How could he permit this endless slaughter, this triumph of evil? Why was he silent? . . . Rouse yourself! Do not forget mankind, your creature! And our cry to God must also be a cry that pierces our very heart, a cry that awakens within us God's hidden presence—so that his power, the power he has planted in our hearts, will not be buried or choked within us by the mire of selfishness, pusillanimity, indifference or opportunism.[1]

Today, there is an "abuse of God's name as a means of justifying senseless violence against innocent persons" and a "cynicism which refuses to acknowledge God and ridicules faith in him. . . . The God in whom we believe is a God of reason . . . not a kind of cold mathematics of the universe."[2]

"Omnia vincit amor," *love conquers all. That is what Virgil wrote in the* Bucolics.

That's right. What Benedict XVI said at Birkenau is that our God is identical with love, with the good. The love of God is stronger. It inspires us with the courage to do the good and to resist evil. An article in the Italian newspaper *La Stampa* bore the title "A Reminder of Evil." So there we are, reminded of evil again. The sad truth is that evil exists, and that there is an evil one who incites us to evil, who tries to bring the world community, world history, to its knees. He is the one behind terrible deeds like the crime perpetrated by Ali Agca.

Fatima happens to be the name of Mohammed's favorite daughter. Now, Vittorio Messori is no rank amateur. When he says or writes something, he knows what he is doing. And he notes that Fatima plays a role for Shiites that is similar to the role of Mary in Catholicism. For instance, Shiite theology assigns Fatima a part in the end-times. The Shiites believe that the Fatima shrine belongs by right to Muslims, and that the Catholics have stolen it from its rightful owners. They argue that if a Lady dressed in shining white appeared there, then it's because she had a message for Muslims, not for Christians. Ali Agca, in his megalomania, thought he had a mission from God. Apparently, when John Paul II visited him at the Rebibbia prison in 1983, he asked the pontiff, "So who is Fatima for you?" Twice now, I've done on-the-scene reporting from Fatima, and both times the cameraman and I have spotted Arabs who seemed to want to remain incognito. They moved quickly as if trying to avoid arousing curiosity or suspicion. We have the pictures to prove it. As you yourself put it at the presentation of the Secret, "Fatima is undoubtedly the most prophetic of modern apparitions."[3] Fatima has a religious and political significance.

Let's stick with the prophecy and not stray into other areas. Instead of contaminating the issue with this kind of stuff, let's shake it off our feet like so much dust. All it does is risk creating confusion and obscuring the true facts. The point you raise is one which I never spoke to Sister Lucia about. Moreover, the CDF has always opposed any attempt to include Muslims among the addressees of the Fatima messages, or even to let them worship in the shrine precincts. The call to penance and conversion is common to all religions, but, in this specific case, the appeal is addressed to the faithful of the Catholic Church. The rest is just wild speculation of a purely earthly nature; there's nothing ethereal or otherworldly about it. Similarly, when I met with Lucia the second time, she showed absolutely no interest in drawing connections between Fatima and the attack on the Twin Towers. We also never discussed sad—but secondary—issues such as the disappearance of Emmanuela Orlandi. The reporters didn't hesitate to ask me about that, either. . . . Please don't tell me you wanted to bring up the Orlandi affair?

Well, in all sincerity I have to admit that the question was on the tip of my tongue. I was about to fall into temptation. Cardinal Agostino Casaroli used to tell me that "the only thing people don't resist is temptation." So now let me ratchet up my sincerity to the level of bluntness. Pope John Paul II applied the Third Secret to himself. This surely didn't make it easy, especially for a Carmelite nun, to take a different position. We are exploring the human story of a pope, but his human story is hard to separate from the supernatural. Moreover, as Gad Lerner has pointed out, John Paul II's story intersects at various points with the crucial narrative line of the twentieth century, that is to say, with an era in which humanity experimented in an unprecedented fashion with the possibility of living as if God didn't exist.

You're looking at Lucia as a kind of competitor with the pope. In your version of the story, she's presented with a fait accompli and bows her head in acquiescence. She feels backed up against a wall and thinks she has no choice but to say yes. I'll let you in on a little secret. During one of the two first meetings, I asked Sister Lucia a question. I don't re-member precisely what I asked; I just put it out of my mind, as you tend to do with useless or unimportant items. I do remember, though, her re-ply, as well as the tone of irritation in which she delivered it: "This isn't a confessional," she snapped. This anecdote reveals her character, the clarity of her convictions, and her freedom. And it gives the lie to those who insistently claim that she was "bought by the Holy Father." Sister Lucia's superior recalls: "No, Sister Lucia's personality was so free that she would never have let herself be bought or influenced by anyone, not even by the pope." Sister Lucia had no previous knowledge of how the pope, Cardinal Ratzinger, or I interpreted the Third Secret. When the three children saw the "Bishop dressed in White," they instinctively per-ceived that it was the pope. Their first spontaneous reaction was to offer prayers for a suffering pontiff. Here, too, the children's perception of things intensified in a kind of crescendo. "Poor Holy Father. We have to pray a lot for him," Jacinta said. Francisco felt the same way: "I pray a lot for sinners so they won't cause the Pope to suffer too much." The hearts of Lucia's two cousins were touched sooner than hers. But prayer, penance, conversion, and the recitation of the Rosary eventually fused into a single experience for the three children, becoming so many facets of one and the same spiritual diamond. When Sister Lucia found out about the shooting, whom did she think of? Her first thought was that the prophecy of the Third Secret had been fulfilled. She thought of John Paul II, and of the unsuccessful attempt on his life. The last piece in a mosaic of suffering was now in place. You see, it's all quite different from the massive carnage certain fevered brains like to imagine taking place, say, in the middle of Saint Peter's Square.

The twentieth century is considered to be the slaughterhouse of history. Tens of millions of Christians were butchered.

You're absolutely right. Millions of Christians were killed. Some, but not all, were Catholics. Plus, in many countries, non-Christians were also slaughtered. The cross was a sign of disgrace, a death sentence. Think of the imprisonment and the tortures, the physical and psychological brutality. When you put it all together, you have a firmament of saints (Pope Benedict XVI spoke of Edith Stein in Auschwitz) who enlighten us like beacons burning brightly in a dark night. When the future Cardinal Văn Thuân was imprisoned, he secretly celebrated Mass at night. Even non-Christians, including his jailers, wanted to receive communion from his hands. Think, too, of Cardinal Todea in Romania or Cardinal Koliki in Albania. They were victims of the effort to eradicate the spirit of friendship with God, to deprive man of the first of his liberties—freedom of religion.

The envelope kept in the CDF bore the title "1960." This was the year when the pope was supposed to open the envelope, as John XXIII in fact did. This date reflected a very definite wish on the part of Sister Lucia.

As the date approached, certain people thought that something extraordinary was bound to happen. I asked Sister Lucia: "Why only after 1960? Was it Our Lady who fixed that date?"[4] She replied: "It was a decision that I took on my own initiative. First, I thought that 1960 lay sufficiently far in the future from when I wrote down the Secret (which was in 1944). Second, I thought I would be dead by then, so that the last obstacle to publishing and interpreting it would be removed. Our Lady didn't tell me anything on this score."[5]

And what do you think?

Sister Lucia's explanation is plausible, but I understand that it may not be completely satisfying. The distance between 1944 and 1960 probably suggested to her mind a remote horizon, a period of time long enough for the meaning of the vision to be understood. It was a fictitious date, and Lucia admitted as much with disarming frankness.

AN ONGOING REVELATION

"When you see a night illumined by an unknown light, know that this is the great sign given you by God that he is about to punish the world for its crimes, by means of war, famine, and persecutions of the Church and of the Holy Father. To prevent this, I shall come to ask for the consecration of Russia to my Immaculate Heart, and the Communion of reparation on the First Saturdays." [1] *We know from contemporary newspaper reports that a spectacular aurora borealis occurred just before the outbreak of World War II. But what else might Mary's dark and threatening words refer to? Perhaps Sister Lucia understood the phrase "consecrate Russia" in the sense of reconsecrating it, rather than simply of erecting a bulwark against Communist ideology, or of converting the Soviet Union from atheism to Catholicism. In any case, the Third Secret stipulates the consecration of Russia as the condition upon whose fulfillment "a period of peace will be granted to the world."* [2]

Now, many people, starting with the Lefebvrites, dream of a Catholic Russia. This dream brings me to a controversy about the validity of the consecration ceremony the pope performed in response to Our Lady's request. In October 2000, for instance, the statue of Our Lady of Fatima traveled to Rome, and John Paul II read out an Act of Entrustment before the image. However, he did not explicitly mention Russia (which was by that time no longer Communist). Nor had he mentioned Russia in his two earlier Acts of Entrustment, which he had performed in 1982 and 1984, respectively. The consecration of Russia obviously posed a very tricky religio-political prob-

lem for Pope John Paul II. The pope, not wishing to offend the sensibilities of our "separated brethren," the Orthodox, remained cautious. An explicit consecration would have been received by the Patriarch of Moscow and All Russia, Alexei II, as a declaration of war. Which of all the Acts of Entrustment most closely conforms to Our Lady's wishes?

I want to make it clear that Lucia didn't conceive of the consecration of Russia as a strategy for capturing this great Christian country for Catholicism. That wasn't the intention of the consecration, which was actually meant to help Russia return to its Christian heritage, to recover its identity as a nation devoted to Our Lady. Remember, the Communist revolution had betrayed and violated Russia's Christian identity, using the might of the state to transform the country into a model of atheism. Although several popes had already entrusted the world to Mary, John Paul II wanted to comply fully with the request Our Lady had made at Fatima. To this end, he composed an Act of Entrustment, which he performed on June 7, 1981. He repeated it in Fatima in 1982. Then, spiritually united with the world's bishops, he closed the Holy Year of the Redemption (1983–1984) with a revised version of the text on March 25, 1984, the feast of the Annunciation. It would be a good idea to reread this prayer of consecration, because the mass media didn't entirely grasp its implications at the time. The Act of Entrustment was entirely in accord with what the Blessed Mother had asked for. Just take the sentence: "Mother of the Church! . . . Enlighten especially the peoples whose consecration and entrustment by us you are awaiting."[3] The reference to Russia is implicit, but it is there. Sister Lucia personally confirmed that this solemn consecration of the whole world satisfied Mary's wishes. "Sim, està feita, tal como Nossa Senhora a pediu, désde o dia 25 de Março del 1984" (Yes, it has been performed, as Our Lady requested, on March 25, 1984). Lucia confirmed Mary's satisfaction in a letter she sent to the pope on November 8, 1989. Any debate about the validity of the Act of Entrustment, or agitation for further acts of consecration, has no leg to stand on. It's true that John Paul II performed another Act of Entrustment in 2000, but it was a prolongation of the one he had made in 1984. His intention was simply to throw the mantle of Mary's maternal protection over the beginning of the new millennium. So Russia has been consecrated, and the consecration was performed on March 25, 1984.

Why did Sister Lucia wait five years to say that Our Lady was satisfied?

I'm convinced that Sister Lucia continued to have conversations, or whatever you want to call them: apparitions, visions, inner locutions, with Our Lady. She had them for decades, all throughout the eighties and beyond. During our meetings, she referred to a whole sequence of dates between 1985 and 1989; it was as if she had been trying to discover from her heavenly interlocutor whether the Act of Entrustment was in accord with God's will. In general, she would wait until she was certain of something before confirming it in writing. But so long as she had the slightest doubt, she preferred to remain silent. Sister Lucia was evasive about her continuing conversations with Mary, and she would change the subject whenever it was brought up. Her community and her prioress, who observed her at close range for decades, came to the conclusion that visions were not at all a rare occurrence with her. The cell of a Carmelite nun holds secrets that the rest of us will discover only in heaven.

I've come to believe, even though I don't have proof, that Sister Lucia wrote several letters to Pope John Paul II. Maybe they are somewhere among the documents that escaped destruction after John Paul's death and are now jealously guarded by his former personal secretary, Cardinal Stanislaw Dziwisz. When John Paul II and Sister Lucia met in Fatima on May 13, 2000, Sister Lucia handed the pope an envelope. What did this envelope contain? We know, or we almost certainly know, that the Czech Bishop Pavel Hnilica, after meeting with the pope shortly before March 25, 1984, clandestinely performed the rite of consecration inside the Kremlin.

I can't resist the opportunity to open a brief parenthesis about Hnilica here. Just three months after his secret ordination to the priesthood, he was made a bishop. Thereupon he himself began secretly ordaining priests, including Jan Korec, who would later become archbishop of Nitra (Slovakia) and a cardinal. Hnilica was also very close friends with Sister Lucia and Mother Teresa of Calcutta. His death in October 2006 ended a life that had all the ingredients of a religious spy thriller. His biography is so gripping that it would make even The Da Vinci Code *pale in comparison. End of parenthesis.*

The years 1983 and 1984 were crucial for relations between the Soviet Union and the West. Russia suspended negotiations over the control of medium-range nuclear missiles. Andropov died, and his successor, Chernenko, passed away just a few months after the 1984 Act of Entrustment. In sum, the Soviet Union found itself in a weakened position on the Euro-Atlantic chessboard. Now, a cloistered nun couldn't possibly be informed about all of these developments. She didn't read military journals, she wasn't on the Reagan administration payroll, and she certainly wasn't in the employ of Western intelligence agencies.

The pope discussed everything openly with Cardinal Ratzinger and myself. I don't know what was in the envelope that Lucia gave John Paul II. As for the late Bishop Hnilica, I share your respect for his unusual life. But the facts you mention occurred during what turned out to be a whole decade of surprises. The Berlin Wall fell on November 9, 1989, and on Christmas 1991 the red flag was lowered for the last time from the highest pinnacle of the Kremlin. Once communism fell apart, the piety of the Russian people, which is saturated with devotion to Mary, reemerged from the catacombs. There was no need to channel it toward Catholicism, and the Slavic pope wisely respected the Russian people's independence. Devotion to Mary was the force that kept the faith of the Russian Orthodox community alive even in the dark years of Communist oppression. So much so, in fact, that when the Soviet Union crumbled it was the youth who poured into the streets, proudly displaying the icons that they had once been forced to keep hidden in their closets or cellars.

FATIMA, THE HOLOCAUST, AND MORE

What value can a prophecy such as Fatima possibly have if it doesn't mention the Shoah, the extermination of the Jews at the hands of the Nazis? Why is the prophecy so lopsided? But now even the hypercritical are satisfied. A recently published booklet for the use of pilgrims to Fatima contains a sort of spiritual diary written by Sister Lucia at the request of the then general of the Carmelite Order, Anastasio Ballestrero, who went on to become cardinal archbishop of Turin. In this diary, Sister Lucia adds an interesting—sensational?—coda to the second part of the message, which predicts that World War I is about to end and warns that another war may break out during the pontificate of Pius XI.

"The war is going to end: but if people do not cease offending God, a worse one will break out during the Pontificate of Pius XI."[1] *In what sense would it be worse? Sister Lucia asks. "In the sense that it would be an atheistic war that attempted to exterminate Judaism, which gave the world Jesus Christ, Our Lady, the Apostles, who transmitted the Word of God and the gift of faith, hope, and charity. The Jews are God's elect people, whom he chose from the beginning: 'Salvation is of the Jews.' " This passage is surprising. Lucia wrote these words in 1955. The text was then sent to Rome by order of Paul VI, where it ended up forgotten in the Vatican Archives (where else?). I won't swear to this, but Sister Lucia's words do sound as if they could be a completion of the Secret as a whole. They report what Our Lady said to Lucia in July 1917. They occur in a memoir* (Come vedo il Messaggio di Fatima nel corso del tempo e degli avvenimenti) *published*

with a foreword by the Discalced Carmelite priest Geremia Carlo Vechina. Three pages later, Lucia adds that God's strength has enabled men to accept change and "has even moved one of the main leaders of atheist communism to travel to Rome to meet with the Holy Father and . . . acknowledge him as God's highest representative . . . to receive the embrace of peace and ask forgiveness for the mistakes of his party." She's obviously referring to the sensational meeting between Mikhail Gorbachev and John Paul II that took place in the Vatican on December 1, 1989. Although Sister Lucia clearly wrote the two passages I've cited at different times and only later reworked them into a single, new text, I confess I am amazed by their content.

What you're saying is something of a surprise to me. They certainly do introduce a new aspect of our topic. They also give us a better insight into how interaction with the supernatural worked in Sister Lucia's life. The words referring to the extermination of the Jews are italicized and appear in quotation marks. This means that Sister Lucia considered them to have a prophetic meaning. So they may be part of the interpretation of the Secret, or perhaps they are a further development of it. In 1955, knowledge about the Shoah was still pretty shaky. It would have been even more confused in a place like Coimbra, where Lucia entered Carmel on March 25, 1948. The horrific discovery of what the Nazis had done, and the ensuing debate about the Holocaust that shook the world's conscience, happened only afterward. Although Sister Lucia knew some theology, she wasn't an academic theologian. She had a supernatural perception of historical facts that made up for what she hadn't learned in the classroom. Her contact with Our Lady was a source of wisdom for her. The statements and observations you cited just now are ones that Lucia kept for herself and that were published only after her death. They certainly deserve a place in her vast body of writings, the fruit of a lifetime dedicated to recounting what had happened to her, first orally and then in writing.

Now, as far as Gorbachev's visit to the Vatican is concerned, it's quite likely that Lucia had learned about it from someone else. And the president of the former Soviet empire may very well have offered the pope a mea culpa. After all, weren't glasnost and perestroika attempts at reform? Wasn't Gorbachev motivated by a noble, if secular, ideal, whose importance was reinforced in his mind by an awareness of the mistakes made by the Soviet Communist Party? How many Russian intellectuals have acknowledged the sins of the Communist regime? Gorbachev was too shrewd not to take responsibility for what had happened in the Soviet Union. If you have an intellectual, or an honest politician, with his back up against a wall, don't forget that he has a brain. Remember, too, that Gorbachev even wrote an article in which he acknowledged the role played by Pope John Paul II in the crumbling of the USSR: "And today we can say that everything that has happened in Eastern Europe in the last few years would not have been possible without the presence of this Pope, without the major role—which was also a political one—that he managed to play on the world scene."[2] "Perestroika" means, among other things, "conversion." The fall of communism happened so quickly and so suddenly. . . . The Communist system seemed invincible, and it looked as if it were going to endure for centuries. But then the whole thing collapsed like a house of cards. The synodal assembly of the bishops (1991) got it right: "even many nonbelievers have seen these events as a sort of miracle."

Cardinal Bertone, we have covered the whole waterfront, or at least almost the whole of it. In spite of that, the ultratraditionalists, the skeptics, and the professionally disappointed secularists will surely be quick with their rebuttals of your testimony. It's practically impossible to eliminate the suspicions that key texts have been doctored. Prejudices are hard to root out. Plus, devotees of the apocalypse need the Secret of Fatima to give their lives meaning and direction. Who knows how many apocryphal writings will continue to circulate under Sister Lucia's name, perhaps even with the spurious legitimation of a copyright? Antonio Socci (this is the "good" Socci who is backing us up here) writes: "What is much more interesting is to reflect on the true mystery, which is not contained in a nun's spartan cell, but in the history that we have all seen with our own eyes." Some people don't want to recognize the prophecy because it eschews political correctness and speaks unflatteringly of communism and atheism. On the other hand, when we look at events such as the October Revolution of 1917, the planetary spread of communism and the grief and ruin that followed in its wake, the unleashing of the Nazi scourge, the Second World War, the attempt on the pope's life, we have to ask ourselves: Are all these things really just a matter of chance? And yet doubt continues to worm its way into our hearts and to gnaw at our minds. In a word: Do the Fatima prophecies contain any new mysteries?

The problem you're describing isn't so much a case of ignorance as it is an expression of invincible stubbornness. I didn't have a tape recorder with me when I met with Sister Lucia, but I did take notes and draft summaries and minutes of the conversations. Lucia read and signed them with full conviction. She wasn't subject to any psychological coercion, and she was in full possession of her mental faculties. I wasn't play-acting with Sister Lucia, and we weren't putting on some carefully staged performance. I went to meet with her in a relaxed setting. I said a few things, and she asked me questions about the pope, the Church, my life, and the Salesians. I spoke with her prioress and the other nuns. Our meetings always took place in a friendly, joyful atmosphere, without the slightest hint of coercion or inquisitorial tactics.

The last time you saw Sister Lucia was on December 9, 2003. You spent five hours with her.

That's correct. The third meeting was a long one, because I celebrated Mass and we thoroughly discussed the issue of Pope John Paul I's part in the prophecy. We've already talked about that at length here. I even shot some photos with Lucia, and she gave me her old cane as a present for the pope. You see, by this time she was confined to a wheelchair, just like the pope. I found this meeting as gratifying as the others. Lucia didn't brood

over her problems, but was full of hope and trust in the Lord. She used to
say: "I have always felt safe under the protection of Our Lord and Our
Lady, who solicitously watches over the pope and the Church." She was
not anxious, but rather radiated calm. She projected a sense of serenity,
punctuated with lively and witty remarks. When her chores were done,
she would retire to the peace of her cell, where she devoted herself to her
own highly personal mission of writing. She had hundreds of letters to
answer, which some of the other sisters would screen for her. One day
they even gave her a computer (though it wasn't hooked up to the Internet). Sister Lucia never worked on a computer, nor did she ever visit a
Web site. She showed a certain interest in the machine, asked some questions, and then concluded: "My machine's better." She was over ninety-
five. This time, our farewell was more tender and more solemn than
usual. Her parting words to me were "You won't see me again; you will
come give me absolution over my body when I am dead."

A prophecy?

In some sense, yes.

And she didn't predict that you would become secretary of state?

(*Laughing.*) No, absolutely not. I had already come a long way, if I
may put it like that. When Sister Lucia died on February 13, 2005, I got a
phone call from the prioress of her convent. A few hours before her
death, Lucia had received a message from John Paul II. Though already
seriously ill himself, the pope had taken the trouble to send his best
wishes to this nun who had come to play such a profound role in his life.
"When Sister Lucia received that letter," the prioress told me, "she acknowledged it as the last great gift of her life. She kept turning it over
and over and wouldn't let go of it." There is also a photo of Lucia in her
last hours. On her nightstand you see the rosary that the pope had given
her for her birthday. After her death, it was returned to the Holy Father.
Though the nuns were reluctant to part with it, they knew that it would

have a special meaning for John Paul II. Sister Lucia's last words were "I offer for the Holy Father, for the Holy Father, for the Holy Father." "At a certain point," the prioress told me, "she opened her eyes, which had so often contemplated the invisible. She looked at all the sisters and then at the crucifix. Then she closed her eyes again. That was her last good-bye." It was 5:25 in the evening. The three shepherds were reunited in heaven. I called Cardinal Ratzinger to tell him that I wished to participate in the funeral as a simple bishop. The next day Cardinal Sodano informed me of the Holy Father's decision to send me to Coimbra as a papal legate. I would preside at the funeral, and at the end of the ceremony I would read a special message from the pope. I immediately informed the papal nuncio in Portugal. When I got to Lisbon, we realized that the message I was supposed to read sounded too Brazilian. Some insisted that the text should be rewritten in literary Portuguese. Once I got to Coimbra, I sought help from the secretariat of state, but, in the end, we decided it would be better to leave the text as it was.

As I said, I presided over the funeral in Portuguese. Well, the Portuguese complimented me on my genuine Portuguese accent. Afterward, some acquaintances e-mailed their condolences from Brazil, and they all expressed their amazement at my perfect . . . *Brazilian* accent. So there you have it: *quidquid recipitur.*

That was a celebration you probably won't forget.

Never. Not only Sister Lucia's convent, but the whole city of Coimbra was covered by a dazzling quilt of white roses. It was as if all the white roses and all the white handkerchiefs in Portugal had found their way to Coimbra. When we emerged from the cathedral, the university students spread out their coats to make a carpet for the funeral procession. There was a huge crowd filled with vibrant faith, a Marian people on pilgrimage. Francis Cardinal Arinze, prefect of the Congregation for Divine Worship and the Discipline of the Sacraments, informed me that authorization had been given to bury Lucia at the Fatima shrine next to the two blesseds, Jacinta and Francisco. But her body was not actually moved to Fatima until 2006. It was Lucia's express wish to be buried in the convent, because she wanted to remain for a while with her sisters. We decided on the spot to respect her wish. And then I blessed the tomb where Sister Lucia was laid.

*

MEDJUGORJE

According to my colleague Saverio Gaeta, if you draw a line between the ten principal sites where Our Lady has appeared in Europe, you get a letter M as in Mary. Now, there are thousands of alleged apparitions, thousands of reports of Madonnas weeping blood. Paul Claudel was exaggerating slightly when he called Fatima "the most important religious event of the century." It makes more sense to argue, as others do, that the Second Vatican Council was the key event of the last century. And yet Mary remains mysteriously present, like the hidden God whom the French novelist François Mauriac writes about. Usually she chooses the simplest people to be witnesses of her appearances: the illiterate, children, the young. As you said earlier, the world is in search of a mother.

After John Paul II was shot, Our Lady allegedly began to appear in Medjugorje. Coincidentally, there is a statue of Our Lady of Medjugorje that reportedly sheds tears of blood in the city of Civitavecchia, not far from Rome. Apparently, it has even done so under the very eyes of the local bishop, Girolamo Grillo. You look thoughtful, Your Eminence; I hope you are not annoyed. One doesn't have to be much of a prophet to guess that Medjugorje won't be recognized easily or soon. On the other hand, there is a basic rule that says that the truth of a supernatural phenomenon is gauged by its fruits, such as prayer, penance, conversion, reception of the sacraments. According to René Laurentin, there are more confessions in Medjugorje than anywhere else in the world. Let's not even talk about the miracles.

The fruits you list are not the sole, or even the primary, criteria. Look, Czestochowa, in Poland, didn't even begin with an apparition recognized by the Church. What you have instead is a Marian shrine that, over the centuries, has borne spectacular fruit. In fact, it has even become the center of Polish national identity. The spirit of an entire people, an entire Catholic people, is continually fed and strengthened there. When I was secretary of the Congregation for the Doctrine of the Faith, I had the job of corresponding with the bishops who requested information and pastoral guidelines regarding Medjugorje.

Did you discourage pilgrimages to Medjugorje?

Not exactly. You see, it's one thing not to organize pilgrimages, and it's another to discourage them. The issue is complicated. In a letter to the French magazine *Famille Chrétienne*, Ratko Perić, the bishop of Mostar-Duvno, made some pretty negative remarks about the presumed supernatural character of the apparitions and revelations at Medjugorje. Perić's letter prompted a request for clarification. In response, the Congregation for the Doctrine of the Faith sent a letter to Gilbert Aubry, bishop of Saint-Denis de la Réunion. It went out on May 26, 1998, under my signature as secretary of the Congregation. In this letter, I clearly laid out our position concerning Medjugorje. First of all, I made a point of clarifying that

> it is not the normal procedure of the Holy See to take a direct position regarding supposed supernatural phenomena before the local authorities have judged in the matter. In all that concerns the credibility of the "apparitions" in question, this dicastery simply defers to the judgment expressed by the bishops of the former Yugoslavia in Zara on April 10, 1991: "On the basis of the investigations made so far, it is not possible to affirm that this is a case of supernatural apparitions or revelations." Since Yugoslavia has in the meantime been

partitioned into several independent nations, the decision to resume any further examination of the issue and, if necessary, to make any new pronouncements on it, would now lie within the competence of the members of the episcopal conference of Bosnia-Herzegovina. Bishop Perić's letter to the editor of *Famille Chrétienne*, in which he writes that "my conviction and position" is not only that "there is no evidence of a supernatural character," but also that "there is evidence of the non-supernatural character of the apparitions or revelations of Medjugorje," must be regarded as the statement of the personal conviction of the bishop of Mostar, who, as the local ordinary, has every right to assert what is and remains his personal opinion. Finally, as far as private pilgrimages to Medjugorje are concerned, this Congregation holds that they are allowed so long as they are not regarded as an authentication of the events taking place there, which still require an examination on the part of the Church.

What pastoral consequences has this had? After all, almost two million pilgrims visit Medjugorje annually. At the same time, not everything has been smooth sailing. For example, the Franciscan friars in charge of Medjugorje's parish church have often been at odds with the local ecclesiastical authorities. Another problem is raised by the imposing mass of "messages" that Our Lady has supposedly entrusted to the alleged seers over the preceding years. And yet former Vatican spokesman Joaquín Navarro-Valls has said: "When a Catholic visits Medjugorje in good faith, he has the right to spiritual assistance."

I'll restrict myself to the important consequences. Bishop Perić's statement expresses a personal opinion of his own. It is not a definitive, official judgment on the part of the Church. The Church defers to the Zara statement issued on April 10, 1991, by the bishops of the former Yugoslavia, and the statement leaves the door open to further investigations of the affair. So the process of verification needs to move forward. In the meantime, private pilgrimages are allowed, and pastors may attend the pilgrims. Finally, all Catholic pilgrims may visit Medjugorje. Medjugorje is a center of Marian piety that provides Catholics a full range of devotional practices in which to express their faith.

If I've got this right, the faithful may be accompanied by priests, but bishops are supposed to keep their distance. Only private pilgrimages are allowed; though, if memory serves, it actually wasn't until 2006 that the Opera Romana Pellegrinaggi responded to Vatican pressure and struck Medjugorje from their list of pilgrimage destinations. I understand that it's necessary to beware of making a religion of apparitions, or of feeding tourism based on such phenomena. I also understand the Church's extreme caution. And yet this remote village in Bosnia-Herzegovina is drawing an increasingly large number of the faithful. During the war in the Balkans, not a single mortar shell or bomb fell on the alleged site of the apparitions. People kept praying and calling on Mary, and all of John Paul II's urgent invitations to peace were heard live at the shrine. But the question everyone is asking is simple: Has Our Lady appeared in Medjugorje or hasn't she?

That is certainly a question mark.

What is your opinion?

The opinion of Tarcisio Bertone is that it is a very big question mark. Medjugorje is to some extent an anomaly that doesn't completely square with other apparitions. It doesn't entirely follow the *traditio,* or tradition, of apparitions. Between 1981 and the present, Mary is supposed to have appeared tens of thousands of times. The volume of Our Lady's alleged messages does not reflect the usual pattern of Marian apparitions, which, like meteors from heaven, tend to have a clear beginning and a clear end. The counterargument, of course, is that the extraordinary times we're living in demand this kind of extraordinary response from Mary. When

I say "the counterargument is," I'm speaking in a roundabout way in order to highlight a certain disagreement I have with this position, which is put forward by folks who want the Church to go in a certain direction. But don't forget that Our Lady is present in all the world's Marian shrines. The purpose of the shrines is to form a sort of spiritual safety net, to be sources of spiritual light, reservoirs of goodness.

You're skeptical and doubtful.

I am with the official Church, though I understand the faithful who go to Medjugorje. I repeat: Extraordinary events aren't absolutely necessary. The manifestation of God through Marian apparitions isn't a sine qua non for the cultivation of a true and authentic devotion to Mary.

IN DEFENSE OF POPULAR PIETY

You have to admit, though, that Fatima continues to attract and intrigue people from wildly different backgrounds: believers and nonbelievers, theocons and devout atheists, Christians and secularists battling for interpretive control of the Enlightenment. Even the head of the Catholic Church, John Paul II, identified himself with Fatima and thus with the devotional practices of popular piety. Now, the combination of popular piety and learned devotion is a rare thing. It is qualitatively different from the spirituality of the ecclesial movements that have flowered in the postconciliar Church. Perhaps we could speak of this fusion of popular piety and learned devotion as a new epiphany, a new Pentecost. It certainly played an unusually large role in John Paul II's life. Indeed, John Paul II embodied it physically in his own existence. After the shooting and the illness it occasioned, the "athlete of God" became the "suffering servant of Yahweh." Is it possible that this transformation happened too quickly, that it too heavily exploited the power of symbolism, or that it substituted the poetry of the exceptional for the—perhaps humdrum—prose of everyday life?

On one hand, religion is already highly symbolic event and reality anyway. It is an integral part of human nature, an essential ingredient of human rationality. While rational*ism* extinguishes the longing for the absolute, genuine human rational*ity* both feeds on symbols and naturally expresses itself in them. On the other hand, the events that took place in the Cova da Iria have been the object of scholarly research; what happened at Fatima has been studied, microscopically scrutinized, and thoroughly analyzed. The shepherd children themselves were subjected to an incessant barrage of interrogations, even by the clergy. Plus, the phenomenon received ample coverage in the Portuguese newspapers of the day.

. Simple believers found a much more direct path to acceptance of the phenomenon. The people of God have a nose for these sorts of things, a kind of sixth sense that should not be lightly dismissed. You see, the terrible cruelty of the twentieth century has forced us to reexamine the foundations of society. Moreover, in our era of globalization, it would be foolish to downplay the importance of an event such as Fatima. Fatima changed history. But it did so by creating more space for the Spirit, which is a dimension of reality that modern society derides or tries to ignore altogether. But the fact that you could fill an entire library with what has been written both about Fatima in particular and about apparitions in general suggests that God is trying to break through the hard shell of our indifference. Apparitions are meant to affect the business of real life, to play a role on the stage of history. This role is intended to challenge both believers and nonbelievers alike. Far from contradicting faith, authentic apparitions lead us to the heart of the Gospel message.

There are certain times in history when it seems that the forces of evil are making a particularly concerted assault on the world. But they never stand unopposed. They must reckon with the resistance of another force, a power of love that upsets or, if you will, derails the course of events. Moreover, love seems to have won. In fact, it *has* won. Admittedly, some have claimed that "Fatima is an embarrassment for believers," that religious categories don't apply to the twentieth century, and that the struggle against authoritarian atheist regimes is not really central to understanding the last hundred years. Similarly, some have asserted that the collapse of communism had nothing to do with the spiritual protest exemplified by John Paul II, and that Western secularism and consumerism were the real bait that lured people away from Marxism, not the yearning to be free for Christian witness. These opinions have the right to be heard in the marketplace of ideas, but they explain at most a part, a segment, an aspect of the whole.

The point I am driving at with all of this is that the purpose behind the revelation of the Third Secret, and of the role John Paul II played in it, was not to stir up the emotions that some people wrongly believe are the real roots of religious experience. Fatima is not a myth but an objective fact and a substantive message that had a real impact on the twentieth century. Both the fact and the message were authoritatively confirmed by Sister Lucia, the only surviving witness, and they were echoed in the intense suffering experienced by Pope John Paul II.

I often have the impression that you are dying to clear up some irritating misunderstanding surrounding Fatima. Both you and Cardinal Ratzinger have been endlessly quoted in newspaper, radio, and TV stories about the revelation of the Third Secret. Both Vatican watchers and other observers have noted that your remarks on the subject tend to sound a note of frustration and dissatisfaction. On the other hand, even experienced journalists such as Luigi Accattoli, Aura Miguel, Marco Politi, Orazio Petrosillo, Marco Tosatti, Andrea Torlnelli, Alceste Santini, Christa Kramer von Reisswitz, and others reveal a certain disappointment of another kind. It is as if they were asking themselves: How can the Third Secret be prophecy that has already been fulfilled? Where is the announcement of the imminent apocalypse? I'm reminded here of the sarcastic comments of critics such as Gianni Vattimo or Sebastiano Vassalli. According to the philosopher Emanuele Severino: "Fatima is a myth that is both ephemeral and anachronistic, because the adversary is no more and we live in a forgetful world. If the coming generations are lucky, they will learn about the titanic clash between the Church and communism in their history or religion classes. But it will be as distant for them as the struggle between the Horatii and the Curiatii is for us."

I know I am not alone in thinking that this sort of judgment entirely misses the point about the Third Secret. The heart of the matter is that John

Paul II elevated Marian devotion to a new status. Devotion to Mary was always recommended by the Church, of course, but it was seen as a kind of extra that believers were free to either accept or reject. John Paul II retrieved the charism of prophecy from undue neglect and restored it to its rightful place in theology, which is faith reflecting intelligently on its own substance.

You've put your finger on the central point, which is faith. Faith has to do with the most radical question of all: "What is man that thou art mindful of him?" (Ps 8:5). Believers are obliged to wrestle with this issue, because part of faith is the attempt to answer the question about the ultimate meaning of things. Through faith, man discovers his infinite value as a *person*. God wishes to enter into communion with man. At the same time, God reveals to man the supernatural end for which he, man, was created: union with God. Saint Ignatius of Antioch says: "I hear in me a living water that murmurs 'Come to the Father.' "

Since Christian Revelation speaks directly to man's natural desire for happiness, the knowledge of what Revelation teaches and the effort to delve more deeply into this teaching are key factors in human happiness as well. John Paul II loved to cite the teaching of Vatican II that man "is the only creature on earth which God willed for itself" (*Gaudium et Spes*, 24). The horizon of our existence is infinite, because it is dynamically ordered to a supernatural goal.

When the religious sense atrophies, superstition quickly steps in to fill the vacuum. It's not that man loses his religious nature. It's that it no longer has a proper outlet, and so it comes out in all sorts of bizarre ways. The result is a proliferation of new forms of psychological slavery. A sophisticated intellectual of the caliber of Claudio Magris has expressed his dismay at what he takes to be a widespread failure to teach the basics of Christianity in general and of Catholicism in particular. Lamenting this ignorance of the fundamentals of religion, this lack of familiarity with the Gospels, he writes: "This is a serious handicap. It is bad for everyone, believers and nonbelievers alike. For Christian culture is one of the greatest, most compelling attempts to work out a grammar for reading, ordering, and representing the world, for giving it meaning and value in our efforts to negotiate the tough and tricky challenge of living."

Some critics have argued that Pope John Paul II pursued a strategy of what they call "meaculpism," a strategy they claim reveals a modernist devil lurking behind the pope's reassuring facade of traditionalism. These critics forget, though, not only that John Paul II was a devotee of Fatima, but also that he encouraged the Congregation for the Doctrine of the Faith to pub-lish Dominus Iesus, *which certain non-Catholic Christians regard as a tombstone placed on the grave of ecumenical and interreligious dialogue. Karol Wojtyla simply didn't fit into the categories of either the Right or the Left. He was from start to finish a politically incorrect pope. A pontiff who embraces Fatima thereby embraces the poster child of a divinely sanc-tioned, militant religiosity. Needless to say, that sort of thing doesn't go down well with theologians who trumpet their own "open-mindedness" and "maturity."*

Dominus Iesus was an answer to numerous letters sent to the pope af-ter the encyclical *Redemptoris Missio.* Missionaries, especially missionar-ies from Asia, were raising questions like these: Nowadays, it seems that anyone, including Mohammed, Buddha, Confucius, and Che Guevara, can be called a "Savior" and put on the same level as Jesus Christ. So what specific task is left for Christian missionaries to fulfill? Why should we spend our lives announcing Jesus's message to the ends of the earth? Obviously, John Paul II was deeply saddened by this disorientation among missionaries—and theologians! So he asked the CDF to prepare a document reaffirming Church teaching that Jesus Christ is the one Savior of the human race. Cardinal Ratzinger oversaw the drafting of the text, but make no mistake: John Paul II was the one who wanted the document written.

The Christological part of Dominus Iesus *met with little resistance. It was the part on the Church that surprised people. The timing also caught the*

*public off guard: The document appeared during the Jubilee year, just as the
pope was dreaming of a meeting on Mount Sinai with the leaders of the
world's great religions, or at least of the three major monotheistic faiths.*

The first three chapters of *Dominus Iesus* set forth Catholic teaching
about Christ as the one Savior of the whole world. The remaining chapters explain the difference between the Catholic Church, on the one
hand, and other churches and ecclesial communities, on the other. People active in ecumenism were unhappy with this second part of *Dominus Iesus,* because they thought it put the brakes on dialogue among
Christians. But we have to see that true ecumenism doesn't mean indis-
criminate acceptance of every theory about the Church. After having
been approved by the cardinal members of the CDF and then by the
pope, the declaration was published on September 6, 2000. The reactions were extremely sharp. At a closed meeting attended by Cardinal
Ratzinger, then-Archbishop Re, and me, John Paul II said: "I want to devote an Angelus address to *Dominus Iesus.* I want to make it clear that
the document was written on my authority and that I'm in perfect
agreement with its message." The pope also decided that he would use
the October 1 Angelus to speak about the declaration. Some of his advisors made the case that he should wait until the Jubilee of the Bishops,
which was scheduled for October 8. When we reminded the Holy Father
of this, he hit the table with his fist and exclaimed: "I've made my decision. The Angelus on *Dominus Iesus* is going to be on October 1, and
that's final." Since Cardinal Ratzinger could not be present in Saint Peter's Square that Sunday, I went in his place.

Were you embarrassed?

Not in the least. It's true that there were some headaches that day, but
they had to do with the canonization of the Chinese martyrs, which had
drawn the ire of the government in Beijing. The declaration, and John
Paul II's Angelus address, simply repeated the teaching of Vatican II, nothing more. *Dominus Iesus* is a string of citations from the Vatican Council.

Karol Wojtyla was a man who challenged and overturned preconceptions, whether it was by the clarity of Dominus Iesus *or by the relish with which he crowned images of Mary all over the world. He was like the author of a huge folk epic whose theme was the celebration of Mary.*

The great theologians, the ones who really believe, are not scandalized by demonstrations of popular piety. Karl Rahner wrote a wonderful little book on devotion to the Sacred Heart of Jesus. It contains some very illuminating passages. Rahner says that the health of any given age depends on whether or not its spirituality can be summed up in the word "heart." For us Christians, of course, this means the "Heart of Christ."

We're going back too far into the past. Maybe we should stick with contemporary theologians.

I'm not interested in making comparisons. My point is that the great thinkers weren't afraid to talk about devotion to the Sacred Heart of Jesus. Rahner comes from a rationalistic school of thought, yet he is able to bring theological depth out of devotion to the Sacred Heart. Cardinal Ratzinger himself wrote a wonderful essay on the same topic, which appeared in his book *Behold the Pierced One.*

Popular piety and rationality seem to make odd bedfellows. In any case, Cardinal Ratzinger administered a healthy dose of rationalism in his theological commentary on the Third Street of Fatima.

Giuseppe de Luca, the famous baritone, has called popular piety a "wisdom of the heart." Ratzinger's theological commentary uses a similar idea as the key to interpreting Fatima:

> This does not mean that a private revelation will not offer new emphases or given rise to new devotional forms, or deepen and spread older forms. But in all of this there must be a nurturing of faith, hope, and love, which are the un-

changing path to salvation for everyone. We might add that private revelations often spring from popular piety and leave their stamp on it, giving it a new impulse and opening the way for new forms of it. Nor does this exclude that they will have an effect even on the liturgy, as we see for instance in the feasts of Corpus Christi and of the Sacred Heart of Jesus. From one point of view, the relationship between Revelation and private revelations appears in the relationship between the liturgy and popular piety: the liturgy is the criterion; it is the living form of the Church as a whole, fed directly by the Gospel.[1]

These remarks go right to the point, I think, in that they suggest a connection between theology and popular piety, public and private revelation.

Some people, though, read them as a sign of instability or imbalance—

Sorry for the interruption, but do you really think Cardinal Ratzinger, today Benedict XVI, is unbalanced when he stops after a walk in the Vatican Gardens to recite the Rosary before an image of the Madonna della Guardia? Look, Pope Benedict is a theologian. In fact, he's one of the greatest theologians of our time.

TWO POPES AND THE ROSARY

We've also seen Benedict praying the Rosary on his way through the Great Saint Bernard Pass, or before the Black Madonna of Altötting, Bavaria's national Marian shrine.

You see, there is nothing outrageous about a great theologian who cultivates simple forms of popular piety. Pope John Paul II used to tell stories of waking up at night and seeing his father kneeling in prayer at the foot of the bed. Cardinal Ratzinger once told me the whole story of Don Bosco and his mother, "Mamma Margherita." He told me about the saint's prophetic dreams and about the games he played with his young charges. The cardinal even knew stories such as the one about Don Bosco and the gray dog. It was Ratzinger's dad, an ex-soldier like Karol Wojtyla's father, who introduced him to this wonderland. But, as pope, the same Ratzinger spoke out in Munich against our

> hardness of hearing . . . where God is concerned . . . Put simply, we are no longer able to hear God—there are too many different frequencies filling our ears. What is said about God strikes us as pre-scientific, no longer suited to our age. . . . We risk losing our inner senses. This weakening of our capacity for perception drastically and dangerously curtails the range of our relationship with reality in general. The horizon of our life is disturbingly foreshortened.[1]

Indeed. I was also struck by the pope's j'accuse against the German church, which eagerly supports the Third World churches when it comes to social work, but not when it comes to evangelization.

Benedict is issuing a warning. He's pointing out that in certain countries the Church is in danger of losing its soul. When that happens, society ends up promoting a totally godless idea of man. In Munich, the pope also stressed that the peoples of Asia and Africa "do not see the real threat to their identity in the Christian faith, but in the contempt for God and the cynicism that considers mockery of the sacred to be an exercise of freedom and that holds up utility as the supreme criterion for the future of scientific research."[2] He then went on to stress the importance of the "fear of God," at which point some of his listeners fell out of their chairs. Such an outmoded expression! What he meant, of course, was "fear of God" in the sense of "respect for what others hold sacred."[3]

The world needs God. But what kind of God?

A good God. In the same homily I have been citing from, Pope Benedict XVI ventured to use some very daring language: "His 'vengeance' is the Cross: a 'No' to violence and a 'love to the end.' This is the God we need. We do not fail to show respect for other religions and cultures, we do not fail to show profound respect for their faith, when we proclaim clearly and uncompromisingly the God who has countered violence with his own suffering; who in the face of the power of evil exalts his mercy, in order that evil may be limited and overcome."[4]

Now that Pope Benedict has a Salesian secretary of state, I suppose he'll try to master all the facts about Don Bosco in order to avoid any embarrassing gaffes.

He already knows almost everything there is to know. I found that out when I accompanied him on a pilgrimage to Valdocco in the district of Turin. His father used to tell him all about Don Bosco. Fancy that: his father.

Let me cite Paul: "For Jews demand signs and Greeks seek wisdom, but we preach Christ crucified, a stumbling block to Jews and folly to Gentiles" (1 Cor 1:22–23). And Jesus says: "Blessed are those who have not seen and yet believe" (Jn 20:29). Is this our normal condition?

Certainly.

The normal condition for everyone?

Well, it's the normal condition for those of us who aren't graced with apparitions, signs, or visions.

Does that include Cardinal Bertone?

Yes, it includes Cardinal Bertone.

Enzo Bianchi of the Bose Community says that what we've called the normal condition is really all we need. The Word of God is enough. According to some statistics, there are about thirty million atheists and over a billion agnostics in the world. A slogan of yesteryear proclaimed the ideal of faith without religion. What we've gotten instead is a multiplication of religions without faith. Nietzsche foretold the "death of God," and others have predicted the eclipse of the sacred. What we are witnessing today, though, is not so much an eclipse of the sacred as it is an eclipse of reason.

That's right. If reason insists on shutting down every opening to the sacred, the result will be an eclipse of reason itself. John Paul II's encyclical *Fides et Ratio* expressed the Church's supreme confidence in reason. The eclipse of the sacred has led to a do-it-yourself approach to the holy, to a kind of supermarket of religious faiths. And, unfortunately, a lot of Catholics are in danger of completely losing their grip on the historical, physical aspect of religion. They'd rather gawk at a weeping Madonna than read a page of the Gospel. They tend to play religious mix and match: Buddhism and Saint Francis, Saint Paul and Zen monasticism. This is Christianity à la carte—you order off the menu in the restaurant of religious experience. A lot of Christians are spiritually naive, and this makes them vulnerable to the influence of superficial ideas and disinformation. By contrast, the act of faith is the only thing that enables you to be reasonable, even though it can at times be inconvenient. Without this *intellectus fidei,* this intelligent understanding of the faith, you end up looking for fake salvation; you end up exhausting yourself in the attempt to be your own redeemer. Without the *cogitatio fidei,* the exercise of thinking "inside" of faith, you end up suffocating under a mass of superstition.

In cauda venenum, *"you've saved the worst for last." Could we say that under Pope John Paul II's leadership the Church survived, but only at the price of wearing itself out? That the Church has been shaken to its foundations, turned upside down, and left in a continual flutter of spiritual activism? You men of the Church have always been like sailors negotiating a rough sea.*

I'll see your Latin and raise you a phrase: *fluctuat nec mergitur,* "tossed by the waves, she does not sink." The Church may be lashed by the stormy sea, but she won't founder. Your question implies a retrospective judgment that I can't agree with. Obviously, John Paul II shook us all up. He didn't leave our hearts undisturbed. At the end of every meeting, he always wanted to come to a conclusion, a practical application. He had the eagerness of an apostle, and it was all-consuming, like a high-explosive bomb.

Would you call it contagious?

Yes, I would. The people he infected most of all were the young. The CDF had to do follow-ups after the publication of certain documents, you know, to monitor reactions. For example, the encyclical *Evangelium Vitae* generated a lot of enthusiastic response throughout the world. The pope got letters from numerous rabbis, from representatives of the major Eastern religions, and from leaders of other Christian churches. On certain issues, issues that meant a great deal to him, he really was the world's spokesman. Karol Wojtyla showed us in his own life what is meant by the "globalization" of faith and values. He embodied both Christian and fundamental human values. John Paul II was the one who brought Sister Lucia out of the shadows and made her a significant player in the drama of our time.

People continue to flood the Marian shrines. Sacred tourism is booming, and there is no letup in sight. But a new shrine has rocketed to the top of the list, a shrine whose popularity stands head and shoulders above the rest: Saint Peter's Basilica, which has become the shrine of Karol Wojtyla. Popular devotion to John Paul II is on its way to overshadowing even the veneration of Padre Pio. Indeed, John Paul II is himself something like the Padre Pio of the third millennium.

Without a doubt. Millions of people became emotionally involved in the events surrounding John Paul II's death. The crowds in Via della Conciliazione and in the adjacent streets of Rome's Borgo Pio were an overwhelming testimony to what this pope had called forth from the depths of the human heart. In the evening, I met with groups of people who had come down from Genoa. After having traveled all night, they waited in line for twelve to fifteen hours for a chance to file past the pope's coffin, and then they returned home on the same day. There were similar groups from all over Italy and abroad. I think Luigi Accattoli sums it up quite well: "In his final days, it was as if we saw the charism of Peter being freed from the constraints of ritual, which had dogged him, both by instinct and by design, throughout his pontificate. This liberation helped him turn his physical disability into a way of communicating with the Church and working to build it up."

THE FASCINATION OF THE DIVINE

At the turn of the millennium, no one on the world stage could speak as effectively on behalf of the world's disinherited as John Paul II. But the pope went a step further: He succeeded in moving the Church beyond its own boundaries and in detaching its identity from Western civilization. After the Wojtyla pontificate, Jesus Christ is no longer European. He is South American, Asian, and African. He is a mestizo with almond-shaped eyes. It took a Polish pope to help the Church become truly universal.

We bishops and cardinals now represent over one hundred different countries from around the world. So all we have to do is look at one another to confirm your point about the universality of the Church. Let me repeat, though, that John Paul II's biggest impact was on youth, and that he reaped his most abundant harvest among them. From 2003 to 2006, I took our diocese's confirmation candidates on an annual pilgrimage to Rome. From 2005 on, the kids would unanimously ask to pray at the tomb of John Paul II in the Vatican Grottoes. Afterward, they would type messages on their cell phones to share their joy with their friends: "I went to the pope's tomb and I cried"; "praying there was the most powerful part of the pilgrimage"; "I'm happy because I saw John Paul again."

Before my departure from Genoa, I received several unexpected applications from young men desiring to enter the seminary. One of the candidates asked to meet with me. During the meeting he said: "Please thank the pope for me. You see, I decided to enter the seminary for two reasons. First, I'm a member of the John Paul II generation and I went to pray at his tomb. Second, I downloaded Pope Benedict's addresses from the Internet. And that's why I'm here." This young man was a recent college graduate with the sure prospect of a bright career. In fact, he had already been hired to fill a bank manager's position. With a big smile on his face, he said: "Today I'm going to meet with the head of human resources and say, 'No thanks, I've decided to give up banking and study for the priesthood.' "

All of us fell in love with John Paul II, but this was especially true of the young (who are also listening attentively to Benedict XVI, by the way). I told Benedict about my meeting with the young man I just mentioned. The pope spoke of it as one of "the spiritual fruits of our time." He also called it one of "the consolations of our time, one of the pope's consolations." We love people who talk about God, people whose lives are filled with him.

Benedict XVI is helping us to change our approach and to see things with new eyes. He's showing us how to stop living *uti Deus non daretur,* as if there were no God, and to start leading lives based on the truth that God exists. We're currently witnessing an explosion of curiosity about the paranormal or parapsychological. People are eagerly exploring new horizons. So why should we marginalize or ignore faith or the Mystery to which faith is the response? Why should we marginalize or ignore this gift of an infinite fullness that enlivens and fulfills human reason? Plato, whom secular critics such as Severino or Vattimo certainly can't fault for being unphilosophical, says in the *Phaedo* that man's highest and most arduous calling is to know the divine nature, and that it would be a fine thing if God should choose to reveal himself to man at some special moment in history. If God should do that, Plato explains, then we would no longer have to rely solely on the fragile raft of reason, because we would know God as he is, face-to-face. Plato's philosophical quest is like a river flowing into the ocean of Revelation, by which I mean the Jewish-Christian Revelation culminating in Jesus Christ. Jesus shows us the

Father. The search for God does not alienate man from himself, so long as he remembers that reason has to remain open to history and so to the Gospel. As Saint Ambrose explains in his treatise *On the Mysteries,* we have to look for God by following the trail of footprints that he himself has left. At a certain point along the way we will bump into a preeminent sign that displays God's unique fingerprint more vividly than any other: the Resurrection of Christ.

It's impossible to encounter Sister Lucia without being touched by her in some way. You were much more than a simple scribe.

Well, my meetings with her greatly reinforced my conviction that it's the simple people who are closest to the heart of God. They're the ones who intercede with God to make the world a better place. If men act humanely, rather than falling into humanity, it's thanks to the prayers of the simple. Another point Sister Lucia brought home to me was the importance of the Rosary, and of the traditions of Christian popular piety in general. I had the good fortune to be born into a rural household where the family said the Rosary and prayed to Our Lady. Our devotion had the same homespun feel as the homemade bread mom used to bake in the oven. We shouldn't underestimate the importance of such practices or try to eliminate them from Christian life.

You officiated at Sister Lucia's funeral. The ceremony didn't generate as much media buzz as, say, Mother Teresa's funeral, not to mention John Paul II's.

Lucia led a hidden life, and to a certain extent the same hiddenness continued after her death. It's silly to make comparisons. The point is not how many people attended the funeral or how many tears were shed. As a matter of fact, the whole of Coimbra marched behind Sister Lucia's casket. Her funeral turned the city into a sea of white roses, an open-air cathedral that rang with stirring music born from the heart of Portuguese religious folk tradition. There were delegations from every part of the planet and a huge media turnout as well.

We have Blessed Jacinta and Blessed Francisco. Why not Blessed Lucia?

I have no doubt that Lucia will also one day be raised to the glory of the altars.

And you will be called upon to give your testimony. Who knows? Maybe even this conversation will further Lucia's cause in some way.

I hope so. And if I am called upon to offer testimony on behalf of Sister Lucia's heroic virtues, I'll be most happy to oblige.

The present prefect of the Congregation for the Causes of Saints, José Cardinal Saraiva Martins, should take note. But let me change the subject for a moment. You are now the number one collaborator of "the world's catechist," Pope Benedict XVI. May we presume that you backed him with full conviction during the last conclave?

Absolutely.

I'm not trying to pry any secrets out of you. The injunction to secrecy is absolute. The last thing we need is an excommunicated secretary of state! I'm guessing, though, that the pope's age—seventy-eight—wasn't an unimportant issue.

Age didn't figure at all. There were precedents. The issue was to determine who at that point was capable of carrying forward the witness of John Paul II and of leading the Church with authority and, of course, God's help. Cardinal Ratzinger had the qualities and the spiritual gravitas which we were looking for.

They call you "the media cardinal." They say you take charge of the field like an aggressive halfback. I suppose we should drop the soccer references, though—especially since your team, Juventus, has dropped down to division B.

Don't forget, though, that it's because of my team that Italy won the World Cup.

I haven't forgotten. What is there in your way of being a priest that reflects Don Bosco and the Salesian charism?

A lot, I would say. The idea of humanity as the basis of every virtue. The Salesian trio: religion, reason, loving kindness. Our founder, Saint John Bosco, used to say: "Even in the worst juvenile delinquents there's a little spark of goodness." So I am an incurable optimist. Everyone has a chance at salvation. It's up to educators and parents to rekindle that little spark and to draw out the positive energies that are hidden in it.

THE CALL OF THE SEA

When you left Genoa for Rome, what did you take with you in your suitcase?

I was the bishop of a historic diocese, whose heart is a city with about 850,000 inhabitants. The Genoese church is very involved in social justice. For example, there are special chaplains for workers, and they have unrestricted access to the premises of all the factories. They meet with the bosses, the workers, and the union leaders. Twice a year, on Christmas and Easter, the archbishop goes to celebrate Mass in the factories and workshops. The current interim archbishop is the chairman of the board of two hospitals: Galliera, which is for adults; and Gaslini, which is for children. So his work takes him where the concerns of the sick, of doctors, and of scientists intersect. Genoa is famous for its socially conscious saints such as Virginia Bracelli and Catherine of Siena. The Genoese have always followed the example of Don Bosco, who focused on youth ministry and care for the needy. Contrary to a lot of stereotypes, the Genoese have always contributed financially to charities such as those founded by Don Bosco, Cottolengo, and Saint Luigi Orione.

What's the thing you most like to remember about your time in Genoa?

Working with young people and celebrating the liturgy in the footsteps of men such as Giacomo Moglia and Abbot Mario Righetti, two pioneers of the preconciliar liturgical reform.

In order to keep alive your Genoese connection, they should name you "Emeritus Pontifical Overseas Legate," since one of your official titles as archbishop of Genoa was actually "legato transmarino," Overseas Legate. Genoa has been a launching pad for you, as it seems to have been for every self-respecting Genoese. After all, the city looks out onto the water, and who can resist the call of the sea?

Genoa is a port city on the edge of the Mediterranean. My own career has swung back and forth between particularity and universality. The pendulum has led me from Rome to Vercelli and back, and then from Rome to Genoa and back. But Genoa, too, has an atmosphere of universality; the Genoese are always looking toward more distant horizons. I'm thinking not only of Christopher Columbus, but also of the Jesuit missionaries, such as the great Spinola, who played a major role in the early evangelization of Japan. In 1992 the diocese of Genoa opened a mission in Santo Domingo. I myself opened one in Santa Clara, Cuba. During my tenure as archbishop, we supported sixty men and women missionaries throughout the world. I always maintained a personal relationship with them, and I always made sure they got their copy of *Il Cittadino,* the diocesan weekly. They may have received it a month late, but that didn't matter. The important thing was that they were not forgotten, because they belonged to a big family. Plus, Genoa was the birthplace of a great pontiff, Giacomo della Chiesa, who became Pope Benedict XV.

The dust of oblivion has settled thickly on Benedict XV. It's a shame, because he was an outstanding pope who did everything he could to defend peace. On August 31, 1914, just three months after he was made a cardinal, he found himself elevated to the papacy. That's an absolute record.

In light of the tragic circumstances of the day, Benedict XV chose to be installed in the Sistine Chapel, rather than in the splendor of Saint Peter's. He became pope at a profoundly sad time for humanity. Austria-Hungary had declared war on Serbia; Germany had declared war on Russia and France; and, after the German invasion of neutral Belgium,

England had declared war on Germany. In short, Europe was in flames. On September 8, 1914, the pope addressed the world's Catholics in his first encyclical. "But as soon as we were able from the height of Apostolic dignity to survey at a glance the course of human affairs," Benedict wrote, "our eyes were met by the sad conditions of human society, and we could not but be filled with bitter sorrow."[1] He also denounced the "useless slaughter" and the "awful butchery staining the honor of Europe." So Benedict XV was a pope of peace. He was farsighted, too. For example, he reorganized the Congregation for the Oriental Churches and created the Pontifical Oriental Institute in Rome. One of his major concerns as a pastor was the missions.

Popes come and go, and so do their "shadows," that is, their secretaries of state. What will be the priorities of Tarcisio Bertone as Benedict XVI's secretary of state? What should we expect?

Perfect accord with the Holy Father, obviously. Furthermore, attention to the crucial issues of our time, especially within the Church, and a vigorous commitment to the new evangelization. Finally, cohesion and unity within the Church, starting with the Roman Curia.

Even the bare outline you've sketched amounts to quite a program. What are the critical issues on the world stage?

One major issue is relations with Islam and China. Pope Benedict also wants us to take concrete steps to improve relations with our brothers in the Orthodox Church. Catholics and Orthodox can't keep appearing before the world so deeply divided.

Your baptism as secretary of state was tough, to put it mildly. It is an experience you are unlikely to forget, given that it happened to coincide with the explosion of the most serious conflict to date between the Vatican and the Muslim world. On September 15, 2006, the very day you stepped into the shoes of your predecessor, Cardinal Angelo Sodano, there were demon-

strations against Pope Benedict XVI in several Muslim countries. These protests were just part of the firestorm of controversy sparked by Professor Emeritus Joseph Ratzinger's now famous Regensburg lecture, which is surely the first scholarly lecture in history to have soured relations between Christianity and Islam (thanks to misleading citations of the text that misrepresented the pope's actual intentions). A lot of Muslim leaders very loudly demanded an apology from the pope, claiming that he had offended the Islamic religion. Here is what Magdi Allam had to say: "It is depressing and alarming to see Muslims, from Bin Laden to the Muslim Brotherhood, from Pakistan to Turkey, from Al Jazeera to Al Arabiya, lining up to form an international front against the pope." At this point, you stepped in and took charge of the situation. You read a long statement. The pope expressed his "regret" that he had been misunderstood, and he received the Arab ambassadors at the Holy See. There was also a powerful symbolism in the fact that Oriana Fallaci happened to pass away at the height of these outrageous attacks on the bishop of Rome.

Yes, that was a time I'll never forget, because I suddenly found myself having to deal with a diplomatic crisis magnified by the media and by the outrage of the Muslim public. It's the toughest challenge that the Vatican has faced in recent memory, and it was certainly the thorniest international controversy at the time. The irony is that the pope was using the Palaeologus passage to make a point about the West. He was arguing for the liberation of reason from its self-imposed confinement to what is experimentally verifiable. He wasn't criticizing Islam but the Western world, which is largely dominated by the belief that only positivist reason, and the sorts of philosophies positivism generates, can claim universal validity. In Regensburg, the pope said that "a reason that is deaf to the divine and that relegates religion into the realm of subcultures is incapable of entering into the dialogue of cultures."[2] This was the context in which he said that "not acting reasonably (σùυ λóγω) is contrary to God's nature."[3] Now, this is a remark that the emperor Manuel II Palaeologus is supposed to have made in a late-fourteenth-century dialogue with a Persian theologian. Benedict referred to his ancient theological debate within a carefully argued, five-page-long lecture. But the journalists reported the Palaeologus citation out of its proper context. Not only was that unprofessional, but it had very serious repercussions, at least initially.

The lines of communication broke down. The media failed to mediate precisely where mediation was the number one priority.

Apropos of the controversy, we shouldn't forget Pope Benedict's words to the Arab ambassadors: "Interreligious and intercultural dialogue is a necessity for building together this world of peace and fraternity ardently desired by all people of goodwill."[4] He went on to say: "In a world marked by relativism and too often excluding the transcendence and universality of reason, we are in great need of an authentic dialogue between religions and between cultures, capable of assisting us, in a spirit of fruitful cooperation, to overcome all the tensions together."[5] Furthermore, in the same speech the pope stressed the special importance of fostering dialogue between Christians and Muslims, and said that "intercultural dialogue between Christians and Muslims cannot be reduced to an optional extra."[6] In fact, he called such dialogue "a vital necessity, on which in large measure our future depends."[7] So you see, the pope has unequivocally declared his commitment to interreligious and intercultural dialogue. It's simply false to claim otherwise.

"Some Journalists Erred" was the headline in the Catholic daily Avvenire. *And the president of the Italian association of the national press, Franco Siddi, pointed a finger at journalists who were "guilty of a serious lapse of professional judgment that has caused incalculable damage to peace and to the image of Benedict XVI."*

Look, let's not get into a discussion of journalistic ethics, which would take us too far afield. The pope's position on Islam, as his apostolic visit to Turkey made abundantly clear, is the same one you find expressed in Vatican II's declaration on the Church's relation to non-Christian religions, *Nostra Aetate:*

> The Church regards with esteem also the Moslems. They adore the one God, living and subsisting in Himself; merciful and all-powerful, the Creator of heaven and earth, who has spoken to men; they take pains to submit wholeheartedly to even His inscrutable decrees, just as Abraham, with whom the faith of Islam takes pleasure in linking itself, submitted to God. Though they do not acknowledge Jesus as God, they revere Him as a prophet. They also honor Mary, His virgin Mother; at times they even call on her with devotion. In addition, they await the day of judgment when God will render their deserts to all those who have been raised up from the dead. Finally, they value the moral life and worship God especially through prayer, almsgiving, and fasting. *(Nostra Aetate,* 3).[8]

In any case, when the Holy See, especially the pope, produces a document on topics such as interreligious dialogue, the relation between religion, war, and violence, you can't skim or, worse, simply ignore them. As I explained to the diplomatic corps, texts such as these require careful reading and meditation. That's the prerequisite for being able to translate their message into practical action capable of conveying to the world the power and pertinence of the Gospel.

A PRAYER IN THE BLUE MOSQUE

The worldwide controversy surrounding the Regensburg lecture under-scores the importance of examining the original sources, instead of taking the media reports at face value. Having learned this lesson, you presented the full text of the lecture, together with the very helpful footnotes, in the October 2006 issue of 30 Giorni, *the monthly magazine edited by Italian senator Giulio Andreotti. Since we live in a climate of forgetfulness, which makes us prone to mistakes and pitfalls, it's worth taking ample time to re-state your argument here.*

I agree. In my presentation of the pope's *lectio magistralis*, I pointed out that Christianity is not confined to the West, and that it can't be identified with Western civilization. At the same time, I stressed that Western democratic civilization needs to forge a dynamic and creative relationship with its own Christian past. Only such a relationship can re-store to the West the drive and initiative, the moral energy, it needs to face the competition on the international scene.

We need to eliminate the anti-Muslim sentiment that many people harbor in their hearts, without of course denying the danger that a lot of Christians currently face in certain Islamic countries. Furthermore, if we want to be credible in our condemnation of the ideological manipula-tion of religion, then we first have to be uncompromising in our con-demnation of the ridicule of religion. We have to speak out against such things as the irreverent caricatures that inflamed masses of people in the Islamic world in 2006. My point is not just that we should respect religious symbols. More simply, and more fundamentally, it's that we have a duty to safeguard the human dignity of the Muslim believer. In a recent discussion about Christian-Muslim relations, a young Italian woman who had converted to Islam said: "For us, the Prophet is not God, but we love him." We need at least to respect such deep feeling.

The criterion governing our dealings with believing Muslims, and even our dealings with terrorists, is not the principle of utility or of harm, but of human dignity. The central objective of the Church's relations with Islam is to promote the dignity of every person and to foster the understanding and protection of human rights. At the same time, we must continue to proclaim the Gospel, even to Muslims, while maintaining the greatest respect for the freedom that is part and parcel of the act of faith.

In your presentation of the pope's lecture, you went on to add that the Holy See was planning to use the apostolic nunciatures in Muslim countries to foster understanding of and, to the extent possible, agreement with the Holy See's position on various issues. You even proposed strengthening relations with the Arab League.

Why be surprised? The Arab League is an international organization, after all. I'd like to underscore the Holy See's intention to foster cultural exchange between Catholic universities and their counterparts in Muslim countries, as well as to facilitate relations between Catholic and Muslim intellectuals on an individual level. Dialogue is possible, I would even say fruitful, when it's conducted in fora such as these. I should also point out that we have organized several international interdisciplinary conferences at the Pontifical Lateran University on topics such as human rights, the notion of the family, justice, and the economy.

I think we need to pursue and intensify this sort of dialogue among Catholic and Muslim intellectuals. We need to be confident that it will eventually trickle down to the masses, where it will change minds and educate consciences. In order to promote this kind of dialogue, the Holy See's communications network has begun sustained efforts to produce more regular Arab-language programming.

Our constant goal in all of this must be to protect the human person as the image of God. Though fragile and under constant assault, the human person is supremely loved by God—loved for his own sake, as Vatican II teaches. This witness to the dignity of the divine image in man is the greatest testimony that the biblical religious traditions can offer to the world.

Shortly after the Regensburg controversy, the pope flew to Turkey, where, among other things, he prayed in Istanbul's Blue Mosque. Afterward, the grand mufti, Mustafa Cagrici, the highest spiritual authority for Turkey's Muslims, said to the pope: "Your prayer is more powerful than your apologies." Cagrici was right: Benedict's visit to the Blue Mosque will go down in the history of the papacy and of Muslim-Christian relations. Indeed, it is almost of greater significance than Pope John Paul II's 2001 visit to the Omayyad Mosque in Damascus. After all, the Omayyad Mosque contains a shrine of John the Baptist. But there was no "Christian interference" in Istanbul during that trip. The live TV coverage was thrilling, to put it mildly. It was an adrenaline rush . . . a spiritual one, of course. Did you also remove your shoes?

Yes, I did, but I didn't put on the white slippers. I entered the Blue Mosque with bare feet.

The grand mufti said to the pope: "Let us take a moment of silence." They were standing in front of the mihrab, the niche facing Mecca. Benedict XVI's hands were folded over his stomach in the position that Muslims refer to as the "prayer of tranquility." Here is how Benedict XVI described this moment of intimate prayer after returning to Rome from the Turkey trip: "Pausing for a few minutes of recollection in that place of prayer, I ad-

dressed the one Lord of Heaven and earth, the Merciful Father of all humanity. May all believers recognize that they are his creatures and witness to true brotherhood!" [1] *You were standing right next to the pope. Did you pray, too?*

Of course. Don't forget that we were in a historic house of prayer, where millions of people have prayed and continue to bring their supplications to the God who is light. Among the many names of God in Islamic theology, this is the one that struck me the most. The calligraphic inscriptions that adorn the walls of the Blue Mosque (some of which were executed by the sultans themselves) proclaim that God is light, and that he is almighty, compassionate, and merciful. Surrounded by such an invitation to praise God's perfections, perfections that Catholic theology also confesses in its own way, why shouldn't one pray? It was impossible not to lift one's heart toward the God of Our Lord Jesus Christ and to ask him to help men of goodwill carry out the great work of building a new world on the foundation of peace. In all of his speeches and meetings in Turkey, Pope Benedict constantly emphasized the word "peace."

How did such a providential decision come about?

In the immediate aftermath of the controversy over the Regensburg lecture, we thought that Rome might be a suitable location for a sign of goodwill and respect toward Muslims. A visit to the city's mosque at the end of Ramadan was one of the possibilities on the table.

Things obviously took a different turn.

We found that there had already been an avalanche of efforts to promote dialogue. There were too many irons in the fire. As we were reviewing the itinerary for the Turkey trip, however, someone pointed out the proximity of the Blue Mosque to the Hagia Sophia and suggested the possibility of a short visit to the former. The pope immediately agreed to the proposal.

The visit to Turkey—the land of Kemal Atatürk, Saint Paul, and Saint John, and the "Meryem Ana," the house of Mary in Ephesus—changed the pope. One could go so far as to say that it transfigured him.

Benedict XVI looked forward to the trip with great serenity of mind. He was totally free of the sorts of fears that some imputed to him. Of course, I'm not denying that we were vigilant, nor am I saying that we went to Turkey with our eyes closed. After all, Advent was just around the corner, and Advent is the season of spiritual vigilance.

In a way, the powerful moment of prayer in the Blue Mosque represented the best of interreligious dialogue. The pope was very pleased with the experience. He had succeeded in getting his message across to the Islamic world. I could sense his delight at having had the opportunity to explain himself to the Muslim masses. He had communicated with millions of believers, opening their consciences for the Holy Spirit to bring about a rapprochement, a change of heart, and a new commitment to the good.

The pope was no longer an enemy, but an ally, because he stood for values assailed by the Babel of sin and perversion known as the modern West. Suddeutsche Zeitung, Germany's biggest newspaper, even went so far as to call Benedict "a pope for Muslims": "Here we have a pope who enters a mosque, looks toward Mecca, and prays next to the grand mufti. If anyone had bet that such a thing would happen, he would have been dismissed as a lunatic."

A lot of clichés are being discarded. The pope has the freshness and spontaneity of a child. He is great because he is simple, because he speaks and reacts with a child's heart. A child's heart that beats in tune with the pulse of the world and, in doing so, resonates with the very heartbeat of God himself.

The same Pope Benedict has also taught us that a person of faith has to have the "courage to provoke."

That's a point he explained during a Wednesday audience from October 2006. Many Christians, he said, "walk in the way of Cain." [1] He was citing the epistle of Jude, which denounces Christians who are like "waterless clouds, carried along by winds; fruitless trees in late autumn, twice dead, uprooted; wild waves of the sea, casting up the foam of their own shame; wandering stars for whom the nether gloom of darkness has been reserved forever." [2]

We're no longer accustomed to such harsh and scathing language.

No, Vatican II teaches us to prefer the high road of dialogue, forgiveness, clemency, and mercy. And yet the pope has warned us not to forget that we have an equal duty to restate and proclaim the main, nonnegotiable distinctions of our Christian identity.

Absolutely. Otherwise we wouldn't be here talking about the crisis of faith or the watering down of Christian identity. To paraphrase Pope John Paul II in Novo Millennio Ineunte: *Christian mediocrity is a recipe for disaster. For example, the dialogue with Islam that everyone is calling for can be fruitful only if we Catholics enter into it with a clear sense of who we ourselves are.*

As you said just now, we need clarity and the courage to provoke. These two values are essential to faith. We need to convince the hesitant. This is why Pope Benedict has been tirelessly recalling us to the beauty of the Christian faith, which is not just a valuable museum piece, or an extra for the culture section of the newspaper. We need to bear witness to the Christian faith, and our testimony must be at once robust and levelheaded. I am delighted that Pope Benedict XVI's first book is about Jesus of Nazareth. "He who sees [Jesus] sees the Father" (Jn 14:9). Benedict's aim in the book is to heal the breach between the "Jesus of history" and the "Christ of faith," a dichotomy, as the pope writes in his preface, that "has penetrated deeply into the minds of the Christian people at large."[3] This is "a dramatic situation for faith, because its point of reference is being placed in doubt: Intimate friendship with Jesus, on whom everything depends, is in danger of clutching at thin air."[4] You see, we have a pope who has lived out his own personal quest for the "face of the Lord," and who is passionate about communicating Christ to others. That's a great example for us. Benedict is an inspiration, not only to theologians, but also to all believers who are ready to take the plunge and to let Christ touch them in a personal way.

It's not easy to coach a team. And your team is so complex, diverse, and varied that any coach would break into a cold sweat at the mere thought of it.

Every new responsibility entails risks. What counts is to have the right intentions. You have to make the most of the resources, talents, and qualities that everyone brings to the team: from the curial staff to the papal nuncios. In particular, you have to rely on the local bishops, who are the pillars of the Church.

The "Benedict revolution" means less diplomacy and politics and more attention to the life of the Church. But the revolution also extends to the pope's personnel decisions. Now we have two theologians at the top.

Benedict is the one who's at the top. I don't consider myself a theologian. I consider myself a scholar who has considerable experience teaching moral theology and canon law. These disciplines have been a help to me. I've also benefited from my contact with bishops and civil authorities from around the world, first as rector of the Salesian Pontifical University and then as secretary of the Congregation for the Doctrine of the Faith. The pope is the theologian here, and my job is to put myself at the service of his mission as universal shepherd of the Church.

I'm convinced that Benedict thought of you for the job of secretary of state as soon as he was elected. And yet the nomination wasn't made until fourteen months after the election. I won't ask you to comment on that. The question I would like to ask is this: How did the pope persuade you to accept the job?

He told me that he wanted me to come to Rome as secretary of state. "Are you sure?" I asked. "Yes, I am sure," he replied. "But there are others who could do a good job." I mentioned a few names. "Yes, I have thought about them, too, but I keep coming back to Cardinal Bertone. So I think the Lord wants him to return to Rome and work with the pope." Benedict then explained his reasons in an open letter to the faithful of the archdiocese.

The pope has spoken of you as a "faithful pastor, especially capable of combining pastoral care and doctrinal wisdom. It is precisely these characteristics, together with the mutual understanding and trust we developed in the years of our common service at the Congregation for the Doctrine of the Faith, that have induced me to choose him for this lofty and delicate task at the service of the universal Church of the Holy See."[5] And he concludes thus: "The history of your diocese shows a generous fidelity to the Vicar of Christ, to which I appeal, also by virtue of the name I chose for my own Petrine ministry: the name of the last Genoese pope, so devoted to Our Lady della Guardia. I entrust everyone to her at this moment of transition, delicate but full of grace, because always 'in everything God works for good with those who love him' " (Rom 8:28).[6]

Truth be told, at the beginning I thought I might be returning to Rome as prefect of the Doctrine of the Faith. That would have been a role more in accord, more in tune, with my training. However, I had only recently arrived in Genoa when the position became vacant after Cardinal Ratzinger's election to the papacy. Since my predecessor, Dionigi Cardinal Tettamanzi, had remained only briefly in Genoa before moving on to Milan, I was sure that I would enjoy a long tenure as bishop, which would allow me to keep working in my own way and at my own pace.

This is surely why Pope Benedict proceeded so cautiously. He didn't rush, but waited for over a year to make the appointment. He must have wanted to soften the impact of yet another bishop's sudden departure from Genoa. You could have said no.

The call came and I said yes. It's true that some people have said "but you should have said no." Okay, but saying no to the pope is the worst thing that a bishop or a cardinal can do. It's especially bad for a cardinal to refuse the Holy Father, because he swears fidelity to the pope *usque ad effusionem sanguinis,* even to the point of his shedding his own blood.

Part Two

Messages, Interpretations, and Acts of Entrustment

THE SECRET OF FATIMA:
PARTS ONE AND TWO OF THE SECRET

*According to the version presented by Sister Lucia in
the Third Memoir for the bishop of Leiria-Fatima (August 31, 1941)
Translated from the original text*

This will entail my speaking about the secret, and thus answering the first question.

What is the secret? It seems to me that I can reveal it, since I already have permission from Heaven to do so. God's representatives on earth have authorized me to do this several times and in various letters, one of which, I believe, is in your keeping. This letter is from Father José Bernardo Gonçalves, and in it he advises me to write to the Holy Father, suggesting, among other things, that I should reveal the secret. I did say something about it. But in order not to make my letter too long, since I was told to keep it short, I confined myself to the essentials, leaving it to God to provide another more favorable opportunity.

In my second account I have already described in detail the doubt which tormented me from June 13 until July 13, and how it disappeared completely during the Apparition on that day.

Well, the secret is made up of three distinct parts, two of which I am now going to reveal.

The first part is the vision of hell.

Our Lady showed us a great sea of fire which seemed to be under the earth. Plunged in this fire were demons and souls in human form, like transparent burning embers, all blackened or burnished bronze, floating about in the conflagration, now raised into the air by the flames that issued from within themselves together with great clouds of smoke, now falling back on every side like sparks in a huge fire, without weight or equilibrium, and amid shrieks and groans of pain and despair, which horrified us and made us tremble with fear. The demons could be distinguished by their terrifying and repulsive likeness to frightful and unknown animals, all black and transparent. This vision lasted but an instant. How can we ever be grateful enough to our kind heavenly Mother, who had already prepared us by promising, in the first Apparition, to take us to heaven. Otherwise, I think we would have died of fear and terror.

We then looked up at Our Lady, who said to us so kindly and so sadly:

"You have seen hell where the souls of poor sinners go. To save them, God wishes to establish in the world devotion to my Immaculate Heart. If what I say to you is done, many souls will be saved and there will be peace. The war is going to end: but if people do not cease offending God, a worse one will break out during the Pontificate of Pius XI. When you see a night illumined by an unknown light, know that this is the great sign given you by God that he is about to punish the world for its crimes, by means of war, famine, and persecutions of the Church and of the Holy Father. To prevent this, I shall come to ask for the consecration of Russia to my Immaculate Heart, and the Communion of reparation on the First Saturdays. If my requests are heeded, Russia will be converted, and there will be peace; if not, she will spread her errors throughout the world, causing wars and persecutions of the Church. The good will be martyred; the Holy Father will have much to suffer; various nations will be annihilated. In the end, my Immaculate Heart will triumph. The Holy Father will consecrate Russia to me, and she shall be converted, and a period of peace will be granted to the world."[1]

SUPPLEMENT TO THE SECOND PART OF THE SECRET: THE SHOAH

The following is taken from a text written by Sister Lucia in 1955 at the request of the father general of the Carmelite order, Anastasio Ballestrero, the future cardinal archbishop of Turin. This "supplement," which is part of a long memoir, was sent to Rome during the pontificate of Paul VI. Sister Lucia undertook a revision of the text sometime after the year 2000. Nevertheless, she was extremely weary and, despite her eagerness to finish the work, she found herself unable to continue. Her superiors assured her that she could stop writing in good conscience, so the work remained incomplete. The memoir was published in its entirety on February 13, 2006, in the book Come vedo il Messaggio di Fatima nel corso del tempo e degli avvenimenti, *with a foreword by Father Geremia Carlo Vechina. The text contains an important addition regarding the Jews, which reads as follows:*

> "The war is going to end." This refers to the 1914–1918 war. "But if people do not cease offending God, a worse one will break out during the Pontificate of Pius XI." In what sense would it be worse? In the sense that it would be an atheistic war that attempted to exterminate Judaism, which gave the world Jesus Christ, Our Lady, the Apostles, who transmitted the Word of God and the gift of faith, hope, and charity. The Jews are God's elect people, whom he chose from the beginning: "Salvation is of the Jews."

FURTHER TEXTS CONNECTED WITH
THE SECOND SECRET

In the Fourth Memoir of December 8, 1941, Sister Lucia writes:

> I shall begin then my new task, and thus fulfill the commands
> received from Your Excellency as well as the desires of Dr.
> Galamba. With the exception of that part of the Secret which
> I am not permitted to reveal at present, I shall say everything.
> I shall not knowingly omit anything, though I suppose I may
> forget just a few small details of minor importance.[1]

Sister Lucia adds:

> In Portugal, the dogma of the faith will always be preserved,
> etc.[2]

THE SECRET OF FATIMA:
THE THIRD PART OF THE SECRET

According to the version presented by Sister Lucia in the Third Memoir for the bishop of Leiria-Fatima (January 3, 1944)

J.M.J.

The third part of the secret revealed at the Cova da Iria–Fatima, on 13 July 1917.

I write in obedience to you, my God, who commands me to do so through his Excellency the Bishop of Leiria and through your Most Holy Mother and mine.

After the two parts which I have already explained, at the left of Our Lady and a little above, we saw an Angel with a flaming sword in his left hand; flashing, it gave out flames that looked as though they would set the world on fire; but they died out in contact with the splendor that Our Lady radiated toward him from her right hand: pointing to the earth with his right hand, the Angel cried out in a loud voice: *"Penance, Penance, Penance!"* And we saw in an immense light that is God: "something similar to how people appear in a mirror when they pass in front of it," a Bishop dressed in White; "we had the impression that it was the Holy Father." Other Bishops, Priests, men and women Religious going up a steep mountain, at the top of which there was a big Cross of rough-hewn trunks as of a cork tree with the bark; before reaching there the Holy Father passed through a big city half in ruins and half trembling with halting step, afflicted with pain and sorrow, he prayed for the souls of the corpses he met on his way; having reached the top of the mountain, on his knees at the foot of the big Cross he was killed by a group of soldiers who fired bullets and arrows at him, and in the same way there died one after another the other Bishops, Priests, men and women Religious, and various laypeople of different ranks and positions. Beneath the two arms of the Cross there were two Angels each with a crystal aspersorium in his hand, in which they gathered up the blood of the Martyrs and with it sprinkled the souls that were making their way to God.

Túy–3–1–1944[1]

THEOLOGICAL COMMENTARY OF THE FORMER PREFECT OF THE CONGREGATION FOR THE DOCTRINE OF THE FAITH, CARDINAL JOSEPH RATZINGER

June 26, 2000

A careful reading of the text of the so-called third "secret" of Fatima, published here in its entirety long after the fact and by decision of the Holy Father, will probably prove disappointing or surprising after all the speculation it has stirred. No great mystery is revealed; nor is the future unveiled. We see the Church of the martyrs of the century which has just passed represented in a scene described in a language that is symbolic and not easy to decipher. Is this what the Mother of the Lord wished to communicate to Christianity and to humanity at a time of great difficulty and distress? Is it of any help to us at the beginning of the new millennium? Or are these only projections of the inner world of children, brought up in a climate of profound piety but shaken at the same time by the tempests that threatened their own time? How should we understand the vision? What are we to make of it? [1]

PUBLIC REVELATION AND PRIVATE REVELATIONS— THEIR THEOLOGICAL STATUS

Before attempting an interpretation, the main lines of which can be found in the statement read by Cardinal Sodano on May 13 of this year at the end of the Mass celebrated by the Holy Father in Fatima, there is a need for some basic clarification of the way in which, according to Church teaching, phenomena such as Fatima are to be understood within the life of faith. The teaching of the Church distinguishes between "public Revelation" and "private revelations." The two realities differ not only in degree but also in essence. The term "public Revelation" refers to the revealing action of God directed to humanity as a whole and which finds its literary expression in the two parts of the Bible: the Old and New Testaments. It is called "Revelation" because in it God gradually made himself known to men, to the point of becoming man himself, in order to draw to himself the whole world and unite it with himself through his Incarnate Son, Jesus Christ. It is not a matter therefore of intellectual communication, but of a life-giving process in which God comes to meet man. At the same time this process naturally produces data pertaining to the mind and to the understanding of the mystery of God. It is a process that involves man in his entirety and therefore reason as well, but not reason alone. Because God is one, history, which he shares with humanity, is also one. It is valid for all time, and it has reached its fulfillment in the life, death, and resurrection of Jesus Christ. In Christ, God has said everything, that is, he has revealed himself completely, and therefore Revelation came to an end with the fulfillment of the mystery of Christ as enunciated in the New Testament. To explain the finality and completeness of Revelation, the *Catechism of the Catholic Church* quotes a text of Saint John of the Cross: "In giving us his Son, his only Word (for he possesses no other), he spoke everything to us at once in this sole Word—and he has no more to say . . . because what he spoke before to the prophets in parts, he has now spoken all at once by giving us the All Who is His Son. Any person questioning God or desiring some vision or revelation would be guilty not only of foolish behavior but also of offending him, by not fixing his eyes entirely upon Christ and by living with the desire for some other novelty" (No. 65; Saint John of the Cross, *The Ascent of Mount Carmel*, II, 22).

Because the single Revelation of God addressed to all peoples comes to completion with Christ and the witness borne to him in the books of the New Testament, the Church is tied to this unique event of sacred history and to the word of the Bible, which guarantees and interprets it. But this does not mean that the Church can now look only to the past and that she is condemned to sterile repetition. The *Catechism of the Catholic Church* says in this regard: "even if Revelation is already complete, it has not been made fully explicit; it remains for Christian faith gradually to grasp its full significance over the course of the centuries" (No. 66). The way in which the Church is bound to both the uniqueness of the event and progress in understanding it is very well illustrated in the farewell discourse of the Lord when, taking leave of his disciples, he says: "I have yet many things to say to you, but you cannot bear them now. When the Spirit of truth comes, he will guide you into all the truth; for he will not speak on his own authority. . . . He will glorify me, for he will take what is mine and declare it to you" (Jn 16:12–14). On the one hand, the Spirit acts as a guide who discloses a knowledge previously unreachable because the premise was missing—this is the boundless breadth and depth of Christian faith. On the other hand, to be guided by the Spirit is also "to draw from" the riches of Jesus Christ himself, the inexhaustible depths of which appear in the way the Spirit leads. In this regard, the *Catechism* cites profound words of Pope Gregory the Great: "The sacred Scriptures grow with the one who reads them" (No. 94; Gregory the Great, *Homilia in Ezechielem* I, 7, 8). The Second Vatican Council notes three essential ways in which the Spirit guides in the Church, and therefore three ways in which "the word grows": through the meditation and study of the faithful, through the deep understanding which comes from spiritual experience, and through the preaching of "those who, in the succession of the episcopate, have received the sure charism of truth" (*Dei Verbum*, 8).

In this context, it now becomes possible to understand rightly the concept of "private revelation," which refers to all the visions and revelations that have taken place since the completion of the New Testament.

This is the category to which we must assign the message of Fatima. In this respect, let us listen once again to the *Catechism of the Catholic Church:* "Throughout the ages, there have been so-called 'private' revelations, some of which have been recognized by the authority of the Church. . . . It is not their role to complete Christ's definitive Revelation, but to help live more fully by it in a certain period of history" (No. 67). This clarifies two things:

1. The authority of private revelations is essentially different from that of the definitive public Revelation. The latter demands faith; in it in fact God himself speaks to us through human words and the mediation of the living community of the Church. Faith in God and in his word is different from any other human faith, trust, or opinion. The certainty that it is God who is speaking gives me the assurance that I am in touch with truth itself. It gives me a certitude that is beyond verification by any human way of knowing. It is the certitude upon which I build my life and to which I entrust myself in dying.

2. Private revelation is a help to this faith, and shows its credibility precisely by leading me back to the definitive public Revelation. In this regard, Cardinal Prospero Lambertini, the future Pope Benedict XIV, says in his classic treatise, which later became normative for beatifications and canonizations: "An assent of Catholic faith is not due to revelations approved in this way; it is not even possible. These revelations seek rather an assent of human faith in keeping with the requirements of prudence, which puts them before us as probable and credible to piety." The Flemish theologian E. Dhanis, an eminent scholar in this field, states succinctly that ecclesiastical approval of a private revelation has three elements: the message contains nothing contrary to faith or morals; it is lawful to make it public; and the faithful are authorized to accept it with prudence (E. Dhanis, *Sguardo su Fatima e bilancio di una discussione,* in *La Civiltà Cattolica* 104 [1953], II, 392–406, in particular 397). Such a message can be a gen-

uine help in understanding the Gospel and living it better at a particular moment in time; therefore it should not be disregarded. It is a help which is offered, but which one is not obliged to use.

The criterion for the truth and value of a private revelation is therefore its orientation to Christ himself. When it leads us away from him, when it becomes independent of him or even presents itself as another and better plan of salvation, more important than the Gospel, then it certainly does not come from the Holy Spirit, who guides us more deeply into the Gospel and not away from it. This does not mean that a private revelation will not offer new emphases or give rise to new devotional forms, or deepen and spread older forms. But in all of this there must be a nurturing of faith, hope, and love, which are the unchanging path to salvation for everyone. We might add that private revelations often spring from popular piety and leave their stamp on it, giving it a new impulse and opening the way for new forms of it. Nor does this exclude that they will have an effect even on the liturgy, as we see for instance in the feasts of Corpus Christi and of the Sacred Heart of Jesus. From one point of view, the relationship between Revelation and private revelations appears in the relationship between the liturgy and popular piety: the liturgy is the criterion; it is the living form of the Church as a whole, fed directly by the Gospel. Popular piety is a sign that the faith is spreading its roots into the heart of a people in such a way that it reaches into daily life. Popular religiosity is the first and fundamental mode of "inculturation" of the faith. While it must always take its lead and direction from the liturgy, it in turn enriches the faith by involving the heart.

We have thus moved from the somewhat negative clarifications, initially needed, to a positive definition of private revelations. How can they be classified correctly in relation to Scripture? To which theological category do they belong? The oldest letter of Saint Paul that has been preserved, perhaps the oldest of the New Testament texts, the First Letter to the Thessalonians, seems to me to point the way. The Apostle says:

"Do not quench the Spirit, do not despise prophesying, but test every-thing, holding fast to what is good" (5:19–21). In every age the Church has received the charism of prophecy, which must be scrutinized but not scorned. On this point, it should be kept in mind that prophecy in the biblical sense does not mean to predict the future but to explain the will of God for the present, and therefore show the right path to take for the future. A person who foretells what is going to happen responds to the curiosity of the mind, which wants to draw back the veil on the future. The prophet speaks to the blindness of will and of reason, and declares the will of God as an indication and demand for the present time. In this case, prediction of the future is of secondary importance. What is essen-tial is the actualization of the definitive Revelation, which concerns me at the deepest level. The prophetic word is a warning or a consolation, or both together. In this sense there is a link between the charism of prophecy and the category of "the signs of the times," which Vatican II brought to light anew: "You know how to interpret the appearance of earth and sky; why then do you not know how to interpret the present time?" (Lk 12:56). In this saying of Jesus, the "signs of the times" must be understood as the path he was taking, indeed it must be understood as Jesus himself. To interpret the signs of the times in the light of faith means to recognize the presence of Christ in every age. In the private revelations approved by the Church—and therefore also in Fatima—this is the point: they help us to understand the signs of the times and to respond to them rightly in faith.

THE ANTHROPOLOGICAL STRUCTURE OF PRIVATE REVELATIONS

In these reflections we have sought so far to identify the theological sta-tus of private revelations. Before undertaking an interpretation of the message of Fatima, we must still attempt briefly to offer some clarification of their anthropological (psychological) character. In this field, theological anthropology distinguishes three forms of perception or "vision": vision with the senses, and hence exterior bodily perception, interior perception, and spiritual vision (*visio sensibilis, imaginativa, intellectualis*). It is clear that in the visions of Lourdes, Fatima, and other places it is not a question of normal exterior perception of the senses: the images and forms that are seen are not located spatially, as is the case, for example, with a tree or a house. This is perfectly obvious, for instance, as regards the vision of hell (described in the first part of the Fatima "secret") or even the vision described in the third part of the "secret." But the same can be very easily shown with regard to other visions, especially since not everybody present saw them, but only the "visionaries." It is also clear that it is not a matter of a "vision" in the mind, without images, as occurs at the higher levels of mysticism. Therefore we are dealing with the middle category, interior perception. For the visionary, this perception certainly has the force of a presence, equivalent for that person to an external manifestation to the senses.

Interior vision does not mean fantasy, which would be no more than an expression of the subjective imagination. It means rather that the soul is touched by something real, even if beyond the senses. It is rendered capable of seeing that which is beyond the senses, that which cannot be seen—seeing by means of the "interior senses." It involves true "objects," which touch the soul, even if these "objects" do not belong to our habitual sensory world. This is why there is a need for an interior vigilance of the heart, which is usually precluded by the intense pressure of external reality and of the images and thoughts that fill the soul. The person is led beyond pure exteriority and is touched by deeper dimensions of reality, which become visible to him. Perhaps this explains why children tend to be the ones to receive these apparitions: their souls are as yet little disturbed, their interior powers of perception are still not impaired. "On the lips of children and of babes you have found praise," replies Jesus with a phrase of Psalm 8 (v. 3) to the criticism of the high priests and elders, who had judged the children's cries of "hosanna" inappropriate (cf. Mt 21:15).

"Interior vision" is not fantasy but, as we have said, a true and valid means of verification. But it also has its limitations. Even in exterior vision the subjective element is always present. We do not see the pure object, but it comes to us through the filter of our senses, which carry out a work of translation. This is still more evident in the case of interior vision, especially when it involves realities that in themselves transcend our horizon. The subject, the visionary, is still more powerfully involved. He sees insofar as he is able, in the modes of representation and consciousness available to him. In the case of interior vision, the process of translation is even more extensive than in exterior vision, for the subject shares in an essential way in the formation of the image of what appears. He can arrive at the image only within the bounds of his capacities and possibilities. Such visions therefore are never simple "photographs" of the other world, but are influenced by the potentialities and limitations of the perceiving subject.

This can be demonstrated in all the great visions of the saints; and naturally it is also true of the visions of the children at Fatima. The images described by them are by no means a simple expression of their fantasy, but the result of a real perception of a higher and interior origin. But neither should they be thought of as if for a moment the veil of the other world were drawn back, with heaven appearing in its pure essence, as one day we hope to see it in our definitive union with God. Rather the images are, in a manner of speaking, a synthesis of the impulse coming from on high and the capacity to receive this impulse in the visionaries, that is, the children. For this reason, the figurative language of the visions is symbolic. In this regard, Cardinal Sodano stated: "[they] do not describe photographically the details of future events, but synthesize and compress against a single background facts which extend through time in an unspecified succession and duration." This compression of time and place in a single image is typical of such visions, which for the most part can be deciphered only in retrospect. Not every element of the vision has to have a specific historical sense. It is the vision as a whole that matters, and the details must be understood on the basis of the images taken in their entirety. The central element of the image is revealed where it coincides with what is the focal point of Christian "prophecy" itself: the center is found where the vision becomes a summons and a guide to the will of God.

AN ATTEMPT TO INTERPRET THE "SECRET" OF FATIMA

The first and second parts of the "secret" of Fatima have already been so amply discussed in the relative literature that there is no need to deal with them again here. I would just like to recall briefly the most significant point. For one terrible moment, the children were given a vision of hell. They saw the fall of "the souls of poor sinners." And now they are told why they have been exposed to this moment: "in order to save souls"—to show the way to salvation. The words of the First Letter of Peter come to mind: "As the outcome of your faith you obtain the salvation of your souls" (1:9). To reach this goal, the way indicated—surprisingly for people from the Anglo-Saxon and German cultural world—is devotion to the Immaculate Heart of Mary. A brief comment may suffice to explain this. In biblical language, the "heart" indicates the center of human life, the point where reason, will, temperament, and sensitivity converge, where the person finds his unity and his interior orientation. According to Matthew 5:8, the "immaculate heart" is a heart that, with God's grace, has come to perfect interior unity and therefore "sees God." To be "devoted" to the Immaculate Heart of Mary means therefore to embrace this attitude of heart, which makes the *fiat*—"your will be done"—the defining center of one's whole life. It might be objected that we should not place a human being between ourselves and Christ. But then we remember that Paul did not hesitate to say to his communities: "imitate me" (1 Cor 4:16; Phil 3:17; 1 Th 1:6; 2 Th 3:7, 9). In the Apostle they could see concretely what it meant to follow Christ. But from whom might we better learn in every age than from the Mother of the Lord?

Thus we come finally to the third part of the "secret" of Fatima, which for the first time is being published in its entirety. As is clear from the documentation presented here, the interpretation offered by Cardinal Sodano in his statement of May 13 was first put personally to Sister Lucia. Sister Lucia responded by pointing out that she had received the vision but not its interpretation. The interpretation, she said, belonged not to the visionary but to the Church. After reading the text, however, she said that this interpretation corresponded to what she had experienced and that on her part she thought the interpretation correct. In what follows, therefore, we can only attempt to provide a deeper foundation for this interpretation, on the basis of the criteria already considered.

"To save souls" has emerged as the key phrase of the first and second parts of the "secret," and the key word of this third part is the threefold cry: "Penance, Penance, Penance!" The beginning of the Gospel comes to mind: "Repent and believe the Good News" (Mk 1:15). To understand the signs of the times means to accept the urgency of penance—of conversion—of faith. This is the correct response to this moment of history, characterized by the grave perils outlined in the images that follow. Allow me to add here a personal recollection: in a conversation with me Sister Lucia said that it appeared ever more clearly to her that the purpose of all the apparitions was to help people to grow more and more in faith, hope, and love—everything else was intended to lead to this.

Let us now examine more closely the single images. The angel with the flaming sword on the left of the Mother of God recalls similar images in the Book of Revelation. This represents the threat of judgment that looms over the world. Today the prospect that the world might be reduced to ashes by a sea of fire no longer seems pure fantasy: man himself, with his inventions, has forged the flaming sword. The vision then shows the power that stands opposed to the force of destruction—the splendor of the Mother of God and, stemming from this in a certain way, the summons to penance. In this way, the importance of human freedom is underlined: the future is not in fact unchangeably set, and the image that the children saw is in no way a film preview of a future in which nothing can be changed. Indeed, the whole point of the vision is to bring freedom onto the scene and to steer freedom in a positive direction. The purpose of the vision is not to show a film of an irrevocably fixed future. Its meaning is exactly the opposite: it is meant to mobilize the forces of change in the right direction. Therefore we must totally discount fatalistic explanations of the "secret," such as, for example, the claim that the would-be assassin of May 13, 1981 was merely an instrument of the divine plan guided by Providence and could not therefore have acted freely, or other similar ideas in circulation. Rather, the vision speaks of dangers and how we might be saved from them.

The next phrases of the text show very clearly once again the symbolic character of the vision: God remains immeasurable, and is the light that surpasses every vision of ours. Human persons appear as in a mirror. We must always keep in mind the limits in the vision itself, which here are indicated visually. The future appears only "in a mirror dimly" (1 Cor 13:12). Let us now consider the individual images that follow in the text of the "secret." The place of the action is described in three symbols: a steep mountain, a great city reduced to ruins, and finally a large rough-hewn cross. The mountain and city symbolize the arena of human history: history as an arduous ascent to the summit, history as the arena of human creativity and social harmony, but at the same time a place of destruction, where man actually destroys the fruits of his own work. The city can be the place of communion and progress, but also of danger and the most extreme menace. On the mountain stands the cross—the goal and guide of history. The cross transforms destruction into salvation; it stands as a sign of history's misery but also as a promise for history.

At this point human persons appear: the Bishop dressed in White ("we had the impression that it was the Holy Father"), other bishops, priests, men and women religious, and men and women of different ranks and social positions. The pope seems to precede the others, trembling and suffering because of all the horrors around him. Not only do the houses of the city lie half in ruins, but he makes his way among the corpses of the dead. The Church's path is thus described as a Via Crucis, as a journey through a time of violence, destruction, and persecution. The history of an entire century can be seen represented in this image. Just as the places of the earth are synthetically described in the two images of the mountain and the city, and are directed toward the cross, so too time is presented in a compressed way. In the vision we can recognize the last century as a century of martyrs, a century of suffering and persecution for the Church, a century of world wars and the many local wars that filled the last fifty years and have inflicted unprecedented forms of cruelty. In the "mirror" of this vision we see passing before us the witnesses of the faith decade by decade. Here it would be appropriate to mention a phrase from the letter that Sister Lucia wrote to the Holy Father on May 12, 1982: "The third part of the 'secret' refers to Our Lady's words: 'If not, [Russia] will spread her errors throughout the world, causing wars and persecutions of the Church. The good will be martyred; the Holy Father will have much to suffer; various nations will be annihilated.' "

In the Via Crucis of an entire century, the figure of the pope has a special role. In his arduous ascent of the mountain we can undoubtedly see a convergence of different popes. Beginning from Pius X up to the present pope, they all shared the sufferings of the century and strove to go forward through all the anguish along the path that leads to the cross. In the vision, the pope too is killed along with the martyrs. When, after the attempted assassination on May 13, 1981, the Holy Father had the text of the third part of the "secret" brought to him, was it not inevitable that he should see in it his own fate? He had been very close to death, and he himself explained his survival in the following words: "it was a mother's hand that guided the bullet's path and in his throes the pope halted at the threshold of death" (May 13, 1994). That here "a mother's hand" had deflected the fateful bullet only shows once more that there is no immutable destiny, that faith and prayer are forces that can influence history and that in the end prayer is more powerful than bullets and faith more powerful than armies.

The concluding part of the "secret" uses images that Lucia may have seen in devotional books and that draw their inspiration from long-standing intuitions of faith. It is a consoling vision, which seeks to open a history of blood and tears to the healing power of God. Beneath the arms of the cross angels gather up the blood of the martyrs, and with it they give life to the souls making their way to God. Here, the blood of Christ and the blood of the martyrs are considered as one: the blood of the martyrs runs down from the arms of the cross. The martyrs die in communion with the Passion of Christ, and their death becomes one with his. For the sake of the body of Christ, they complete what is still lacking in his afflictions (cf. Col 1:24). Their life has itself become a Eucharist, part of the mystery of the grain of wheat that in dying yields abundant fruit. The blood of the martyrs is the seed of Christians, said Tertullian. As from Christ's death, from his wounded side, the Church was born, so the death of the witnesses is fruitful for the future life of the Church. Therefore, the vision of the third part of the "secret," so distressing at first, concludes with an image of hope: no suffering is in vain, and it is a suffering Church, a Church of martyrs, which becomes a signpost for man in his search for God. The loving arms of God welcome not only those who suffer like Lazarus, who found great solace there and mysteriously represents Christ, who wished to become for us the poor Lazarus. There is something more: from the suffering of the witnesses there comes a purifying and renewing power, because their suffering is the actualization of the suffering of Christ himself and a communication in the here and now of its saving effect.

And so we come to the final question: What is the meaning of the "secret" of Fatima as a whole (in its three parts)? What does it say to us? First of all we must affirm with Cardinal Sodano: "the events to which the third part of the 'secret' of Fatima refers now seem part of the past." Insofar as individual events are described, they belong to the past. Those who expected exciting apocalyptic revelations about the end of the world or the future course of history are bound to be disappointed. Fatima does not satisfy our curiosity in this way, just as Christian faith in general cannot be reduced to an object of mere curiosity. What remains was already evident when we began our reflections on the text of the "secret": the exhortation to prayer as the path of "salvation for souls" and, likewise, the summons to penance and conversion.

I would like finally to mention another key expression of the "secret" that has become justly famous: "my Immaculate Heart will triumph." What does this mean? The heart open to God, purified by contemplation of God, is stronger than guns and weapons of every kind. The *fiat* of Mary, the word of her heart, has changed the history of the world, because it brought the Savior into the world—because, thanks to her *Yes,* God could become man in our world and remains so for all time. The Evil One has power in this world, as we see and experience continually; he has power because our freedom continually lets us be led away from God. But since God himself took a human heart and has thus steered human freedom toward what is good, the freedom to choose evil no longer has the last word. From that time forth, the word that prevails is this: "In the world you will have tribulation, but take heart; I have overcome the world" (Jn 16:33). The message of Fatima invites us to trust in this promise.

Joseph Cardinal Ratzinger
Prefect of the Congregation
for the Doctrine of the Faith

JOHN PAUL II'S ACT OF ENTRUSTMENT TO
THE IMMACULATE HEART (MARCH 25, 1984)

"Como Nossa Senhora a pediu"
(As Our Lady requested)

Pope John Paul II had already performed an Act of Entrustment in Fatima on May 13, 1982. He repeated this gesture on March 25, 1984, the feast of the Annunciation. Spiritually united with the world's bishops, he entrusted the earth's inhabitants to the Immaculate Heart of Mary. The Holy Father raised his voice in solemn supplication, begging God to liberate mankind from hunger, war, and every evil. He added a special request that Mary would enlighten those peoples whom she herself had asked to be consecrated and entrusted. What follows is the text of the March 25, 1984, Act of Entrustment to Our Lady:[1]

"We have recourse to your protection, holy Mother of God."

As we utter the words of this antiphon with which the Church of Christ has prayed for centuries, we find ourselves today before you, Mother, in the Jubilee Year of the Redemption.

We find ourselves united with all the pastors of the Church in a particular bond whereby we constitute a body and a college, just as by Christ's wish the Apostles constituted a body and college with Peter.

In the bond of this union, we utter the words of the present Act, in which we wish to include, once more, the Church's hopes and anxieties for the modern world.

Forty years ago and again ten years later, your servant Pope Pius XII, having before his eyes the painful experiences of the human family, *entrusted and consecrated to your Immaculate Heart* the whole world, especially the peoples for which by reason of their situation you have particular love and solicitude.

This *world of individuals and nations* we too have before our eyes today: the world of the second millennium that is drawing to a close, the modern world, our world!

The Church, mindful of the Lord's words "Go . . . and make disciples of all nations . . . and lo, I am with you always, to the close of the age" (Mt 28:19–20) has, at the Second Vatican Council, given fresh life to her awareness of *her mission in this world.*

And therefore, *O Mother of individuals and peoples,* you who know all their sufferings and their hopes, you who have a mother's awareness of all the struggles between good and evil, between light and darkness, which afflict the modern world, accept the cry that we, moved by the Holy Spirit, address directly to your Heart. *Embrace,* with the *love* of the Mother and Handmaid of the Lord, this human world of ours, which we entrust and consecrate to you, for we are full of concern for the earthly and eternal destiny of individuals and peoples.

In a special way we entrust and consecrate to you those individuals *and nations* that particularly need to be thus entrusted and consecrated.

"We have recourse to your protection, holy Mother of God": *despise not our petitions in our necessities.*

Behold, as we stand before you, Mother of Christ, before your Immaculate Heart, we desire, together with the whole Church, to unite ourselves with the consecration which, for love of us, your Son made of himself to the Father: "For their sake," he said, "I consecrate myself that they also may be consecrated in the truth" (Jn 17:19). We wish to unite ourselves with our Redeemer in this his consecration for the world and for the human race, which, in his divine Heart, has the power to obtain pardon and to secure reparation.

The power of this consecration lasts for all time and embraces all individuals, peoples, and nations. It overcomes every evil that the spirit of darkness is able to awaken, and has in fact awakened in our times, in the heart of man and in his history.

How deeply we feel the need for the consecration of humanity and the world— our modern world—in union with Christ himself! For the redeeming work of Christ must be *shared in by the world through the Church.*

The present year of the Redemption shows this: the special Jubilee of the whole Church.

Above all creatures, may you be blessed, you, the Handmaid of the Lord, who in the fullest way obeyed the divine call!

Hail to you, who *are wholly united* to the redeeming consecration of your Son!

Mother of the Church! Enlighten the People of God along the paths of faith, hope, and love! Enlighten especially the peoples whose consecration and entrustment by us you are awaiting. Help us to live in the truth of the consecration of Christ for the entire human family of the modern world.

In entrusting to you, oh Mother, the world, all individuals and peoples, *we also entrust to you this very consecration of the world,* placing it in your motherly Heart.

Immaculate Heart! Help us to conquer the menace of evil, which so easily takes root in the hearts of the people of today, and whose immeasurable effects already weigh down upon our modern world and seem to block the paths toward the future!

From famine and war, *deliver us.*

From nuclear war, from incalculable self-destruction, from every kind of war, *deliver us.*

From sins against the life of man from its very beginning, *deliver us.*

From hatred and from the demeaning of the dignity of the children of God, *deliver us.*

From every kind of injustice in the life of society, both national and international, *deliver us.*

From readiness to trample on the commandments of God, *deliver us.*

From attempts to stifle in human hearts the very truth of God, *deliver us.*

From the loss of awareness of good and evil, *deliver us.*

From sins against the Holy Spirit, *deliver us.*

Accept, Oh Mother of Christ, this cry *laden with the sufferings* of all individual human beings, *laden with the sufferings* of whole societies.

Help us with the power of the Holy Spirit to conquer all sin: individual sin and the "sin of the world," in all its manifestations.

Let there be revealed, once more, in the history of the world the infinite saving power of the Redemption: the power *of merciful Love!* May it put a stop to evil! May it transform consciences! May your Immaculate Heart reveal for all the *light of Hope!*

CHRONOLOGY OF THE EVENTS OF FATIMA

March 30, 1907: Lucia is born in Aljustrel, a tiny hamlet in the parish of Fatima, to Antonio and Maria Rosa dos Santos.

March 11, 1908: Francisco Marto, Lucia's cousin, is born.

June 10, 1910: Francisco's sister, Jacinta Marto, is born.

1915: An angel appears to Lucia, Francisco, and Jacinta as they tend the flocks.

1916: The angel appears a second and third time to Lucia and her two young cousins. The angel declares his identity: "I am the Angel of Portugal, the Angel of Peace."

May 5, 1917: Benedict XV, faced with the unfolding tragedy of the First World War, decides to add the invocation "Queen of Peace, pray for us" to the Litany of Loreto: "So let this loving and devout appeal rise toward Mary, the Mother of Mercy who is omnipotent by grace. . . . Let it bring to Her ears the anguished cries of mothers and wives, the lament of innocent children, and the sighs of every generous heart. May her most tender and benevolent concern be touched, and may she grant the peace that we request for this troubled world."

May 13, 1917: Our Lady appears for the first time in the Cova da Iria. The three shepherd children are invited to return to the same spot on the thirteenth of each of the following months.

May 13, 1917: Benedict XV performs the episcopal ordination of Eugenio Pacelli, the future Pope Pius XII.

July 13, 1917: The Virgin delivers her message, but asks the children not to reveal it. The next apparition occurs on August 19.

October 13, 1917: The "Miracle of Sun" occurs before tens of thousands of witnesses. The lady clothed in light reveals that she is Our Lady of the Rosary.

April 4, 1919: Francisco Marto dies in his family home in Aljustrel.

February 20, 1920: Jacinta Marto dies in Dona Stefania Hospital.

1920: Lucia moves to Lisbon.

June 16, 1921: On this day, Lucia is favored with what could be considered a seventh apparition of Our Lady. Lucia is about to begin her education in the town of Vilar (near Porto), in a school directed by the Dorothean Sisters. Lucia herself will later enter the Dorothean order, assuming the religious name of Maria dos Dores.

October 1925: Lucia arrives in Pontevedra, Spain, where she begins her postulancy as a Dorothean. Her real wish is to enter the Carmelite convent in Lisieux, but she already has trouble enough with Spanish, and her inability to learn French forces her to abandon hopes of entering the Lisieux Carmel. She remains a Dorothean sister for twenty-seven years.

December 10, 1925: Lucia receives what would become known as the "Great Promise of the Immaculate Heart of Mary." The promise includes the call to offer the five first Saturdays in reparation for the offenses committed against the Sacred Heart.

October 1926: First official visit of the Bishop of Fatima to the Cova da Iria.

June 13, 1929: Lucia is visited by new apparitions in the Dorothean chapel in Túy, Spain. These are followed by further apparitions between March 29 and 30, 1930.

1930: The commission appointed by Bishop Correia to investigate the genuineness of the Fatima apparitions presents its findings. The bishop thereupon publishes a pastoral letter containing the following statement: "After having consulted with the Reverend Counselors of this diocese, and humbly invoking the Holy Spirit and the protection of the Most Holy Virgin, we hereby declare on the strength of the arguments set forth here, as well as of others that we omit for the sake of brevity, that the visions seen by the shepherd children between May 13 and October 13, 1917, in the Cova da Iria, located in the parish of Fatima in this diocese, are worthy of faith. We also hereby authorize the official cult of Our Lady of Fatima."

January 25, 1938: An extraordinary aurora borealis is seen over a great part of Europe. Lucia regards it as a sign given by God that a new war is about to begin.

December 2, 1940: Lucia writes to Pius XII and expresses her wish to reveal Our Lady's message. The pope does not answer.

August 31, 1941: Lucia writes down the first two parts of the Secret.

December 8, 1941: Lucia adds a few annotations to the first two parts of the Secret.

December 8, 1942: Pius XII consecrates the war-torn world to the Immaculate Heart of Mary in Saint Peter's.

January 3, 1944: Lucia writes the third part of the Secret.

March 25, 1948: At 5:30 in the morning, Lucia enters the Carmel of Saint Teresa in Coimbra. Her new religious name is Sister Maria Lucia of Jesus and the Immaculate Heart. She is forty years old.

October 30, 1950: Two days before the proclamation of the dogma of the Assumption, Pius XII witnesses a mysterious phenomenon while walking in the Vatican gardens: "The sun, which at that point was rather high in the sky, had the appearance of a yellow globe surrounded by a halo of light. There was a small cloud in front of it. The light, however, did not prevent me from gazing sunward with perfect ease. The opaque globe was moving slightly, now spinning, now swaying from left to right and vice versa. The interior of the globe was visibly shaken by continuous violent convulsions. The same phenomenon happened again on the following day, October 8; on November 1, the day of the definition [of the Assumption]; and, finally, on November 8, the octave of the solemnity. As of the time of this writing, however, it has not occurred again. On a number of separate days following these events, though always at the same time and in the same, or very similar, atmospheric conditions, I tried to look at the sun to see if the phenomenon would repeat itself. My efforts, however, were in vain, because I could not keep my eyes fixed on the sun for even a moment without being immediately blinded by its light. This is the pure truth, which I have tried to relate as briefly and simply as possible."

The similarities with the "dance of the sun" on October 13, 1917, are obvious.

October 13, 1951: Federico Cardinal Tedeschini is sent as papal legate to close the Holy Year in Fatima.

1955: In the final part of the Second Secret, Lucia adds an explicit reference to the extermination of the Jews. She speaks of an atheistic war leading to the Shoah.

April 4, 1957: The sealed envelope containing the Secret is brought to the secret archives of the Holy Office. Sister Lucia is informed of this action by the bishop of Fatima.

August 17, 1959: The commissary of the Holy Office, Father Pierre Paul Philippe, O.P., brings the sealed envelope containing the Third Secret to John XXIII. The pope's reply: "Let us wait. I will pray. Then I will let you know what I have decided." John XXIII's decision is to keep the message secret.

March 27, 1965: Paul VI reads the Third Secret with the deputy secretary of state, Angelo Dell'Acqua. The pope's secretary, Pasquale Macchi, also reads it. Paul VI decides not to publish the text and sends the envelope back to the archives of the Holy Office.

May 13, 1967: Paul VI is welcomed in Fatima by a million people waving white handkerchiefs. He briefly meets with Sister Lucia outside the basilica. In September 1967, the pope receives a letter from the visionary.

July 11, 1977: The patriarch of Venice, Albino Cardinal Luciani, has a long conversation with Sister Lucia in her convent in Coimbra. To this day there is speculation about whether or not she foretold his election to the papacy.

May 13, 1981: The unprecedented shooting of John Paul II at 5:19 in the evening in Saint Peter's Square by the Turkish assassin Ali Agca. The shooting occurs on the anniversary of the first of Our Lady's six apparitions in Fatima.

July 18, 1981: Cardinal Franjo Seper, prefect of the Congregation for the Doctrine of the Faith, delivers two envelopes (a white one containing Sister Lucia's original Portuguese text of the Third Secret and an orange one with the translation of this text) to the deputy secretary of state, Archbishop Eduardo Martínez Somalo. The two envelopes are brought to the ninth floor of the Gemelli Clinic in Rome, where the pope is recovering from the assassination attempt. John Paul II reads the Third Secret. On August 11, the two envelopes are brought back to the archives of the Holy Office.

May 13, 1982: Pope John Paul II makes a pilgrimage to Fatima to thank Our Lady, convinced that she has rescued him from death.

December 27, 1983: John Paul II meets with Ali Agca in Rome's Rebibbia prison. Ali Agca remains strangely unaffected by the pope's offer of forgiveness, and speaks instead of the uncanny elements surrounding the pontiff's connection with Fatima.

March 25, 1984: John Paul II performs a solemn Act of Entrustment in which he consecrates the world to the Immaculate Heart of Mary. The text contains an implicit reference to Russia, whose consecration Lucia had repeatedly requested: "Enlighten especially the peoples whose consecration and entrustment by us you are awaiting."[1] Lucia confirms the validity of this act of consecration: "Yes, it has been done, as Our Lady asked, on March 25, 1984." Never before had a pope gone so far in publicly complying with the request of a visionary in his capacity as head of the universal Church.

May 13, 1990: John Paul II returns to Fatima. There is a growing expectation that the Third Secret will be revealed. The pope meets with Sister Lucia, who continues to have visions of Our Lady in her cell.

April 27, 2000: Tarcisio Bertone meets with Sister Lucia for the first time. The pope has decided to publish the Third Secret, but he needs Lucia to confirm the genuineness of the document and the interpretation of the message. Does the Third Secret refer to the shooting of John Paul II? Lucia's answer is affirmative. The "Bishop dressed in White" is indeed Pope John Paul II.

May 13, 2000: Jacinta and Francisco are beatified in Fatima by John Paul II. At the end of the beatification ceremony, the secretary of state, Cardinal Angelo Sodano, alludes to the content of the Third Secret.

June 26, 2000: The veil is removed from the greatest mystery of the twentieth century. The Third Secret is presented and explained at a press conference in the Vatican Press Room. The presenters are Cardinal Joseph Ratzinger, prefect of the Congregation for the Doctrine of the Faith, and the secretary of the CDF, Archbishop Tarcisio Bertone.

November 17, 2001: Archbishop Bertone's second meeting with Lucia. The issue is once more the genuineness of the text of the Third Secret published by the Vatican. Has everything been revealed? Have there perhaps been some glaring omissions? And why does the commentary refer to Sister Lucia's Third Memoir, and not to the Fourth? Sister Lucia cuts to the chase: "Everything has been published; there are no more secrets."

December 9, 2003: Tarcisio Bertone, now a cardinal, meets for the third and final time with Sister Lucia. During their long conversation, they discuss the role of Albino Luciani, if any, in the Third Secret. Lucia says nothing concerning the rumors of her alleged prophecy that Luciani would have a short and painful pontificate. Instead, she signs a summary of her conversation with Luciani that he himself published a few months before his election to the papacy. Lucia is still lucid, but she feels the end drawing near. She tells Cardinal Bertone that they will not meet again, and that the Cardinal will come to her funeral.

February 13, 2005: At 5:25 in the afternoon, Sister Lucia breathes her last. She is ninety-seven. Her death marks the passing of a woman who has had a profound impact on the century that we may justly call the "century of Mary."

February 15, 2005: Lucia, the last seer of Fatima, is buried in Coimbra. Cardinal Tarcisio Bertone officiates at the funeral service. In 2006 Sister Lucia's body is entombed in the basilica of Fatima next to her two beatified cousins, Jacinta and Francisco.

FAREWELL TO THE READER

In honor of Sister Lucia, Sister Maria Celina of Jesus Crucified, the prioress of the Carmelite convent in Coimbra, wrote a prayer that nicely captures the personality of this "saint in progress." I would like to cite Sister Maria Celina's prayer as a simple, prayerful farewell to the reader:

Even in old age, she remained
One of the little ones Jesus calls blessed.
She was a gift: a crystal fountain
That sang cheerfully in the midst of tears!

She suffered throughout her life the secret pain of
Exile from the Heaven
That she had once glimpsed!
She first had to become a child again,
As she was when she saw
Our Lady!

She was Heaven's faithful confidante, and
When at last she surrendered her weary body,
Her Mother came to take her home!

She will not forget us in Paradise.
She watches us with her smile,
She walks at our side!

NOTES

FOREWORD

1. *L'Osservatore Romano,* English edition, June 28, 2000, p. viii.
2. Ibid.
3. http://www.vatican.va/holy_father/benedict_xvi/letters/2007/documents/ hf_ben-xvi_let_20070222_present-bertone_en.html.

A NOTE TO THE READER

1. http://www.vatican.va/gpII/documents/homily-card-ratzinger_20050408_ en.html.
2. From Bernanos's *Diary of a Country Priest.*

INTRODUCTION

1. http://www.vatican.va/holy_father/benedict_xvi/angelus/2006/documents/ hf_ben-xvi_ang_20061001_en.html
2. http://www.vatican.va/holy_father/benedict_xvi/angelus/2006/documents/ hf_ben-xvi_ang_20061001_en.html
3. *Paradiso,* V, 76–78.
4. *Maria: Nuovissimo Dizionario* (Bologna: Edizioni Dehoniane, 2006), 22.
5. As per the official Vatican text of the Third Secret; see below.
6. The quotes are from the official Vatican texts of the three parts of the secret; see below.

Part One: A RADIANT, CREDIBLE WITNESS

1. http://www.vatican.va/roman_curia/congregations/cfaith/documents/ rc_con_cfaith_doc_20000626_message-fatima_en.html

THE TRANSFORMING POWER OF FATIMA

1. As per the official Vatican text; see below.
2. *Come vedo il Messaggio di Fatima nel corso del tempo e degli avvenimenti* (Coimbra: Edizioni Carmelo di Coimbra—Segretariato dei Pastorelli, 2006), 17.

JOHN PAUL II: THE POPE OF THE THIRD SECRET

1. Pope John Paul II, *Meditation from the Policlinico Gemelli to the Italian Bishops,* May 13, 1994; cited at http://www.vatican.va/roman_curia/congregations/cfaith/documents/rc_con_cfaith_doc_20000626_message-fatima_en.html
2. As per the official Vatican text; see below.
3. http://www.vatican.va/roman_curia/congregations/cfaith/documents/rc_con_cfaith_doc_20000626_message-fatima_en.html

ONE ENVELOPE, ONE SECRET

1. As per the official Vatican text; see below.

MYSTERIES BEYOND OUR KEN

1. http://www.vatican.va/holy_father/benedict_xvi/speeches/2006/may/documents/hf_ben-xvi_spe_20060528_auschwitz-birkenau_en.html
2. http://www.vatican.va/holy_father/benedict_xvi/speeches/2006/may/documents/hf_ben-xvi_spe_20060528_auschwitz-birkenau_en.html
3. http://www.vatican.va/roman_curia/congregations/cfaith/documents/rc_con_cfaith_doc_20000626_message-fatima_en.html
4. Ibid.
5. This does not quite square with what is on the official Web site, which reads thus: "It was not Our Lady. I fixed the date because I had the intuition that before 1960 it would not be understood, but that only later would it be understood. Now it can be better understood. I wrote down what I saw; however it was not for me to interpret it but for the Pope"; http://www.vatican.va/roman_curia/congregations/cfaith/documents/rc_con_cfaith_doc_20000626_message-fatima_en.html

AN ONGOING REVELATION
1. As per the official Vatican text; see below.
2. As per the official Vatican text; see below.
3. http://www.vatican.va/roman_curia/congregations/cfaith/documents/
   rc_con_cfaith_doc_20000626_message-fatima_en.html

FATIMA, THE HOLOCAUST, AND MORE
1. As per the official Vatican text; see below.
2. The same passage is cited in Dziwisz book.

IN DEFENSE OF POPULAR PIETY
1. As per the official Vatican text; see below.

TWO POPES AND THE ROSARY
1. http://www.vatican.va/holy_father/benedict_xvi/homilies/2006/
   documents/hf_ben-xvi_hom_20060910_neue-messe-munich_en.html
2. Ibid.
3. Ibid.
4. Ibid.

THE CALL OF THE SEA
1. http://www.vatican.va/holy_father/benedict_xv/encyclicals/documents/
   hf_ben-xv_enc_01111914_ad-beatissimi-apostolorum_en.html
2. http://www.vatican.va/holy_father/benedict_xvi/speeches/2006/september/
   documents/hf_ben-xvi_spe_20060912_university-regensburg_en.html
3. Ibid.
4. http://www.vatican.va/holy_father/benedict_xvi/speeches/2006/september/
   documents/hf_ben-xvi_spe_20060925_ambasciatori-paesi-arabi_en.html
5. Ibid.
6. Ibid.
7. Ibid.
8. http://www.vatican.va/archives/hist_councils/ii_vatican_council/documents/
   vat-ii_decl_19651028_nostra-aetate_en.html

A PRAYER IN THE BLUE MOSQUE

1. http://vatican.va/holy_father/benedict_xvi/audiences/2006/documents/
hf_ben-xvi_aud_20061206_en.html

"AS A CARDINAL, I COULDN'T SAY NO"

1. http://www.vatican.va/holy_father/benedict_xvi/audiences/2006/documents/
hf_ben-xvi_aud-20061011_en.html
2. Ibid.
3. English translation, p. xii.
4. http://www.vatican.va/holy_father/benedict_xvi/audiences/2006/documents/
hf_ben-xvi_aud_20061011_en.html
5. http://www.vatican.va/holy_father/benedict_xvi/letters/2006/
documents/hf_ben-xvi_let_20060622_fedeli-genova_en.html
6. Ibid.

Part Two: THE SECRET OF FATIMA: PARTS ONE AND TWO OF THE SECRET

1. http://www.vatican.va/roman_curia/congregations/cfaith/documents/rc_
con_cfaith_doc_20000626_message-fatima_en.html

FURTHER TEXTS CONNECTED WITH THE SECOND SECRET

1. http://www.vatican.va/roman_curia/congregations/cfaith/documents/rc_
con_cfaith_doc_20000626_message-fatima_en.html
2. Ibid.

THE SECRET OF FATIMA: THE THIRD PART OF THE SECRET

1. http://www.vatican.va/roman_curia/congregations/cfaith/documents/rc_
con_cfaith_doc_20000626_message-fatima_en.html

THEOLOGICAL COMMENTARY

1. http://www.vatican.va/roman_curia/congregations/cfaith/documents/rc_
con_cfaith_doc_20000626_message-fatima_en.html

JOHN PAUL II'S ACT OF ENTRUSTMENT TO THE IMMACULATE HEART

1. The Vatican Web site http://www.vatican.va/roman_curia/congregations/ cfaith/documents/rc_con_cfaith_doc_20000626_message-fatima_en. html)

CHRONOLOGY OF THE EVENTS OF FATIMA

1. As per the official Vatican text; see below.

For complete original documents please visit www.vatican.va